Blue Collar Conservatives

Blue Collar Conservatives

RECOMMITTING TO AN AMERICA THAT WORKS

Rick Santorum

REGNERY
PUBLISHING

A Salem Communications Company

Library of Congress Control Number: 2014934158

ISBN 978-1-62157-239-8

Published in the United States by
Regnery Publishing
A Salem Communications Company
Washington, DC
www.Regnery.com

Manufactured in the United States of America

10 9 8 7 6 5 4 3 2 1

Books are available in quantity for promotional or premium use. Write to Director of Special Sales, Regnery Publishing, One Massachusetts Avenue NW, Washington, DC 20001, for information on discounts and terms, or call (202) 216-0600.

Distributed to the trade by
Perseus Distribution
250 West 57th Street
New York, NY 10107

Blue Collar Conservatives is dedicated to
all the hardworking moms and dads who both
pursued their dreams and sacrificed them for their children
to forge the greatest country in the history of the world.

To Karen, Elizabeth, John, Daniel, Sarah Maria, Peter,
Patrick, and Bella for helping me with this book.
You are my American Dream.

CONTENTS

INTRODUCTION

It was a night I will never forget, November 6, 2012. Another election night, something we had experienced a dozen times throughout the 2012 Republican primary season, only this time we were actually rooting for Mitt Romney to win. I sat with my wife, Karen, and our children at home waiting to see if the exit polls we had seen earlier in the day were going to play out. I felt uncomfortable not being in the action, but mainly I felt frustrated that the two campaigns ended up fighting over mostly minor issues, distracting America from the questions that made this the most consequential election since the Civil War.

Dramatic, dangerous changes are taking place in America, and this election should have been about them. One such change is a fundamental restructuring of Washington's relationship with the American people. Our freedom as individuals, families, businesses, and communities is being drastically curtailed by imperious bureaucrats who think they know better than we do how to run our lives. The botched implementation of Obamacare has given us a glimpse of what happens when these grand government schemes inevitably fail. People get hurt.

In 2012, so much was at stake, yet so little was debated. For more than a century, the growing left wing of the Democratic Party has been pursuing a secularist and socialist agenda for America. Their method is class warfare—pitting one group of Americans against another. It's the rich versus the poor, men versus women, the 1 percent versus the 99, the insurance company versus the uninsured, and the natural gas driller versus his neighbors. They don't want to improve on America's success, correct its mistakes, and help it live up to its promise. They think that something is wrong with America at its core—that it needs to be "fundamentally transformed."[1] Their progress was slow but steady until they achieved their breakthrough in 2008 with the election of Barack Obama and supermajority Democrat control of both houses of Congress.

After four years of unchecked "transformation," Americans should have had a chance for second thoughts. But President

Obama's opponent was the wrong choice to lead the charge against the Democrats' radical agenda. Governor Romney is as fine a man as I know. I supported him for president in 2008. But I also knew that in 2012, the political climate was very different. The challenger to President Obama couldn't be a wealthy financier who supported the Wall Street bailouts at a time when the "Occupy" movement and the president had successfully created a narrative for Middle America of the 99 percent versus the 1 percent. Even worse than a nominee who would be on the defensive against the president's greatest weapon, class warfare, Romney was, as I often repeated during the campaign, "uniquely unqualified"[2] to press our best argument against the president—Obamacare. As governor of Massachusetts, he signed the law that paved the way for Obamacare, the focal point of a conservative movement that rallied the country in 2010 to a historic victory in the House of Representatives.

That is why Karen and I decided that I should run for president. I felt called to make the case that the establishment candidate could not win on both Obamacare and the 99 percent. I would campaign as a grandson of immigrants who didn't come from money. I would campaign for the working man. I would campaign on America's first principles of faith, family, freedom, and opportunity, which are the antidote to President Obama's secular statism.

What kept me in the race as I sat at the bottom of almost every national poll were the people I met, particularly in the early caucus state of Iowa. I visited all ninety-nine counties and did about 381 town hall meetings and speeches in that state over the course of 2011. The average attendance at these local gatherings was about twelve, including me, so I really got to know people. What struck me was their passion and concern for our country. They encouraged me to keep fighting, because they believed what I believed.

———

The conventional wisdom in the spring of 2012 was that President Obama would be defeated.[3] The economy was stagnant. "Hope and change" had provided no hope and only change for the worse. In a contest between Obama and "anybody but Obama," Obama was going to lose.

The pundits, as it turned out, were wrong. "Anybody but Obama" wasn't good enough. It mattered whom the Republicans nominated from both a policy and personal perspective. The critical swing voters—middle- and lower-middle–income Americans from industrial and rural communities with generally conservative values—swung for Obama or stayed home. Ironically, they were the ones who were being hurt the most by Obama's failed economic policies. They generally don't look to the government for help. But our party didn't seem to care about them. After four years of economic insecurity, what hope did we offer them that they would be better off with a Republican president?

Mitt Romney's résumé as a venture capitalist didn't help him here. I defended him in the primaries when others were attacking his Wall Street deals, because people like him create efficient and profitable companies. Venture capitalists nurtured Apple, Intel, and Google. And there's nothing wrong with making money and living well in America. Mitt Romney is a great businessman, problem solver, and manager, and I can't fault him for running on his strengths.

But those strengths played into Obama's hands in 2012. The Democrats and their allies in the media were determined to turn the election, using the politics of envy, into the decisive battle of the great class war. And the Republican establishment obliged by nominating what turned out to be the perfect opponent.

———

After the election, many Americans were polled on why they voted as they did. Out of all the data and analyses, one fact jumped out at me: those who voted for a candidate because he "cared more" about people like them chose President Obama over Governor Romney by a margin of *63 percent*.[4] Even if you win the argument on political philosophy, leadership, and managerial competence, it's hard to win an election when most voters don't think you care about them.

As filtered through the media, Romney was wrongly portrayed to America as an aloof Wall Street millionaire—like the guy "who fired your dad," as Jon Stewart put it.[5] Obama, by contrast, was the one who cared. The Americans I met all across the country were worried about the economy, the pace of change in the workplace, and the coarsening culture. They liked it when the president talked about their plight, but they didn't like his remedy of government handouts. Romney offered the solutions that Republicans have espoused for more than thirty years: cut taxes, slash government, and everyone will be fine. Low taxes and lean government are good macroeconomic policy, but it's hard for ordinary people to see how that policy will affect them and their families. Republicans like to quote John F. Kennedy's observation that "a rising tide lifts all boats,"[6] but Romney never got across how he would help the people—and there are millions—whose boats are full of holes.

In my campaign for president, I traveled to corners of this country that national politicians rarely visit, including rural communities with double-digit unemployment. I was down on the Gulf Coast where they are still recovering from Katrina and in the mill towns of Michigan, Ohio, and Wisconsin where manufacturers are fighting for their lives against foreign competition and a hostile federal government. I was in the oil and gas fields where they're drilling as fast as they can in the fear that President Obama might shut them down. That's what he did to the coal towns I visited in Ohio, West Virginia, and Illinois.

The folks I heard from most in my travels were hardworking Americans worried about losing their jobs. Their towns are the America I grew up in and where I've spent most of my life. This is the proud America that once thrived and is now tragically broken and largely forgotten in today's political debates. In these places, millions of blue-jeaned workers have been left behind and see little hope for the future. Skilled laborers who once had good salaries and pensions now seek part-time jobs at big-box retail stores or have even been enticed onto public assistance.

I talked to many people on the campaign trail who just want to hear there is still opportunity for a good life in America. They seek some stability and security for themselves and opportunity for their children to go to good schools, get decent jobs, and build families of their own. They want reassurance that despite all of the terrible economic news and pain, the American Dream is still alive for them. It seems to them that neither party hears them. They don't want more government benefits, and they don't want to work sixteen hours a day, seven days a week, to grab the brass ring at the top of some corporation or firm. They want someone out there to lift up the people who work a shift, go home to volunteer at the animal shelter, church, or PTA, spend time with their families, and enjoy their leisure time. They want someone to recognize that they are just as important to the success of our economy and culture as the entrepreneur or corporate executive who puts in all of his time at work. We must be the party for them, because America will fail without them.

The United States must do everything it can to nurture the inventors and entrepreneurs who are the creative spirits of our free economy, and here the case for Republican policies is strong. But that's not enough. We Republicans must show the unemployed, the underemployed, and the struggling worker that we are on their side and want their support. We cannot forget the blue collar conservatives who are the back-bone of this country. We have an obligation to restore the American Dream for them and their families. And until we internalize this as a party, we will continue to lose national elections.

=====

Republicans are waking up to some startling new realities in American politics. The demographic profile that propelled them to victory in five out of six presidential elections from 1968 to 1988—white and married voters—is an ever-smaller portion of the population. If the ethnic and racial composition of the United States were the same as it was in 1992, Mitt Romney, who carried the white vote by more than 20 percentage points, would have beaten Barack Obama in a landslide. We've been using a badly outdated playbook.

My friend and former colleague at the Ethics and Public Policy Center Peter Wehner has assembled for his fellow conservatives a mound of demographic and electoral data that makes our political challenges stark and unmistakable.[7] "Republicans," he concludes, "at least when it comes to presidential elections, have a winning message for an electorate that no longer exits."

The minority share of the vote in 2012 was 28 percent, more than twice what it was when Bill Clinton was elected in 1992.[8] If the minority share of the vote reaches 30 percent of the total in 2016, as expected, and if the Democratic candidate carries 80 percent of that vote, the Democrat will need only 37 percent of the white vote to win.[9]

I don't like electoral calculations based on race, and I'm happy to leave racial politics to the other side. The American Dream should be color-blind, and so should our politics. The fact remains, however, that unless the Republican Party broadens its appeal to minorities, its prospects are grim.

Still, the Republicans didn't lose the presidential election of 2012 only because blacks and Hispanics and Asians voted against them. As many as six million blue collar voters stayed home from the polls, and there's good reason to believe that a large majority of them would have voted Republican if they had voted.[10] Those voters—many of them in the rural and small-town Rust Belt—didn't hear anything in the Republican message to inspire their confidence in our party to make their lives better. If anything, they detected a note of contempt.

The demographer Joel Kotkin, a refreshingly clear-eyed observer of American politics though by no means a conservative, offers the best advice to the Republican Party I've heard: remember Lincoln. Kotkin scolds us for having "confused being the party of plutocrats with being the party of prosperity," and I think he's closer to the truth than we'd like to admit. The first Republican president, Abraham Lincoln, came from the ranks of working Americans and pursued an economic agenda that had their interests at heart. Whether it was expanding the country's railroads or passing the Homestead Act, his policies "helped people achieve their aspirations."[11]

If we really become the party of opportunity for working Americans, we'll go a long way toward solving the problem of minority voters' estrangement from us. The elites of the Democratic Party, I'm sorry to say, have raised the politics of racial and ethnic division to an art form. The way for Republicans to win the votes of minorities is not to out-pander the Democrats but simply to appeal to them as working Americans who want to take part in the American Dream—a dream that shouldn't be the exclusive property of Ivy Leaguers and investment bankers.

———

Restoring the American Dream does not mean going back in time. Conservatives are often criticized for their romanticized view of the good old days prior to the culture shock that was the 1960s. Having said that, let's make no mistake about it—the greatest threat to the average American's achieving his dream today is a dysfunctional culture. To heal our nation, we must promote the ideals upon which American culture has thrived for over two centuries—ideals based on timeless truths. Our challenge is to redeem and recommit to the timeless truths that set America on a course to greatness and to formulate policies consistent with those truths in a world that has changed dramatically since World War II.

This book is all about what we as a party and a movement can do to help the blue collar conservatives, working Americans trying to set things right for their families, their communities, and their country.

CHAPTER ONE

BLUE COLLAR CONSERVATIVES REALLY DID BUILD IT

There was a time not long ago when Americans without college degrees could expect to earn a decent and steady income in exchange for hard work. This income and job stability provided a foundation for families and communities that, with their churches, Little Leagues, Boy Scout troops, and a hundred other civic organizations, fostered the strong values and the work ethic that underpinned American life. Millions of Americans came of age in these communities and took those values with them as they started their own families and thanked God for his blessings.

With good incomes, Americans could afford new cars, kitchen appliances, and trips to Disneyland. Demand for such new goods kept others working and employment strong. With stable marriages, children enjoyed the gift of security and neighborhoods where values were taught at home and in church and enforced by parents.

This is how I grew up. My grandparents came here from Italy in 1930, fleeing fascism and settling in a coal town in the hills outside of Johnstown, Pennsylvania. That's where they found freedom and the opportunity to earn decent pay for hard work in the mines. They found a gritty but overall wholesome place to raise their kids and taught them that in America there was no limit to what they could become. I know the American Dream was real because my grandparents lived it.

Their son Aldo, my father, was seven when his family left Italy for America. He served in the U.S. Army Air Corps in the South Pacific in World War II, and when he came home from the war, he earned advanced degrees in clinical psychology. He worked for the Veterans Administration (now the Department of Veterans Affairs) counseling World War II, Korea, and Vietnam vets for almost forty years. At his first post, in Martinsburg, West Virginia, he met and married my mother, Catherine, an administrative nurse. I was born in 1958, the second of three children. Unlike most mothers at that time, my mother continued to work as a nurse. It was a great setup because the hospital where she worked was a stone's throw from our house. My siblings and I spent our childhoods living in various rented World War II–era buildings, including the post jail that had been converted into apartments. When I was seven, we returned to western Pennsylvania and settled in Butler, among the mines and steel furnaces that were the economic bedrock of that part of the country.

I went to Butler Catholic Grade School and then Butler High School. Like other kids, I played (but not well) both baseball and basketball, and I saw my first major league game, between the Pittsburgh Pirates and the Cincinnati Reds, at Forbes Field. As in most small towns in America back then, families kept their doors unlocked. Kids roamed neighborhoods freely, but there was always a parent nearby, and they didn't hesitate to enforce the values of the community. And though I wasn't aware of this at the time, this world was possible in part because Butler made stuff. While my dad didn't work in the mill, almost all of my friends' dads did. That and numerous school field trips to local plants drove home the importance of manufacturing to our community. We had thriving manufacturers like the Pullman-Standard Company, which made railroad cars (it was shuttered in the 1980s and demolished in 2005), and an Armco steel plant, which is now AK Steel. There was a job for virtually anyone out of high school who was willing to work an honest day. And those jobs carried benefits and security that formed the core of the community. Looking back, it's not a very complicated equation.

Those field trips and conversations with my friends' dads were extra motivation for me, and many others, to hit the books in school. It was clear then that change was afoot with automation and global competition, so I headed off to Penn State University, where I fell in love with Penn State Nittany Lions football, drank my share of Rolling Rock beer (after I turned twenty-one, of course), and found my vocation in politics and public service. I worked on campaigns and ended up founding the College Republicans club on campus.

After Penn State, I got an MBA degree from the University of Pittsburgh, worked for a couple of years, went back to law school, and became an attorney in Pittsburgh. Three years later, I met my future wife, Karen Garver, who was a neonatal nurse and law student. In 1990, at age thirty-one, I left my law firm to run for Congress, serving two terms in the House of Representatives before running for the U.S. Senate. In all, I represented Pennsylvania in Congress for sixteen years, from 1991 to 2007. And during those years, Karen and I had eight children. We gave them the basics: the security of a good marriage, our time schooling them at home, and faith in our Lord and Savior.

=====

I've gone pretty far on the steel-town values of education, working hard, loving your family, and living your faith. That doesn't mean that we've never had problems. We've had more than our share, but my family, and our neighbors, schoolmates, teammates, and church members, has shared a common belief that we needed to look out for one another and be there when we were needed. Getting help from the government wasn't something you wanted—or wanted anyone to know that you had—and you took it only when you absolutely needed it. And even then, you didn't take it for very long.

There are remnants of that America in some small towns and tight-knit neighborhoods. But my travels during the presidential campaign have sadly reminded me that many of the jobs that were once the basis of those communities for the 70 percent of Americans who don't have college degrees are all but gone. Over the past few decades, bad corporate and labor leadership, a growing regulatory burden, and competition from low-wage countries have made America less competitive and jobs harder to come by. Economists turn this reality into statistics and tell us that we're moving from a manufacturing to a service economy and that while the old jobs are gone, new ones will come. But with those old jobs gone, the toll has been more than economic; its effect on families and communities has been devastating.

———

Much has been made of a January 2014 study by a group of distinguished economists from Harvard and the University of California at Berkeley that appears to refute the common perception that it's harder to get ahead in America than it used to be.[1] Examining forty years of data on economic mobility and inequality, the Equality of Opportunity Project found that "[c]hildren entering the labor market today have the same chances of moving up in the income distribution (relative to their parents) as children born in the 1970s."[2] Republicans, however, should resist the temptation to dismiss all the talk about declining mobility as another hyped-up crisis—like global warming—and settle back to our old economic policies. For one thing, upward mobility varies greatly from community to community in America. Not surprisingly, it's the lowest in rural and depressed areas. The poorest kids in San Francisco, Washington, D.C., and Salt Lake City, for example, are more than twice as likely to reach the highest income percentiles as those in Dayton, St. Louis, and Charlotte. And while our economic mobility rate has not changed substantially over time, it is lower than in other developed countries. Think about that—in upward mobility, the Land of Opportunity is falling behind the rest of world.

Digging a little deeper, the study reveals that globalization and automation in manufacturing and the breakdown of families and communities—circumstances that contribute to economic inequality—have been counterbalanced by a healthier environment, technological advancements that produce better living standards, and more opportunities for women and minorities. But ever-increasing automation and the additional loss of jobs to global competition are without question steepening the incline for lower-educated and lower-skilled workers, particularly men, and their families.

When I campaigned for president in 2012, I was pigeonholed by the media as the "social conservative" candidate who only talked about abortion, marriage, and, of all things, contraception. Anyone who actually bothered to show up to one of those 381 town hall meetings in Iowa or any of my hundreds of other talks around the country would know what an inaccurate characterization that was. But my coming out of nowhere with no money to win the Iowa caucuses, where social conservatives make up a large percentage of the vote, reinforced that caricature. What the uninformed "experts" sitting in New York and Washington didn't realize was that my stance on moral issues didn't differentiate me from the field. It was how I integrated those issues into the central discussion of improving our economy.

In a debate at Dartmouth College in New Hampshire, I got the chance to take that message to a national audience. I explained that the word "economy" comes from "oikos," the Greek word for family. The family is the first economy, and healthy marriages lead to financial success and stability in an overwhelming percentage of cases. It's no coincidence that the Equality of Opportunity Project concluded that family structure was the most important determinant of upward mobility. Children raised in single-parent households are the least likely to climb the ladder of success, followed by children raised in two-parent families who live in communities of mostly single parents.

Today, marriage rates are at a historical low while illegitimacy is at a historical high.[3] And just as marriage—an institution older than any government and the foundation of a stable society—has fallen into this crisis, activist courts are redefining it in a way that extinguishes whatever meaning it had left. Let me be clear—I am not blaming the breakdown of marriage and the family on the same-sex marriage movement. The sexual revolution has been taking a jackhammer to that foundation for fifty years. No one would be talking about same-sex marriage if we had not lost the real meaning and purpose of marriage years ago.

Working Americans are now finding fewer and fewer of the opportunities that we once took for granted. Sure, they might find a good job in the lumber department at Home Depot or driving a delivery truck for FedEx, but long-term, steady employment opportunities—the kind that can support a family—appear to be gone for many Americans. In too many towns, the disappearance of quality jobs has brought not only economic hardship but a host of social pathologies, from alcohol and drug abuse to petty crime, obesity, and dependence on welfare. The teenage mother, the drug addict, or the convicted felon who emerges from these circumstances will find few opportunities to escape a life of poverty. It's a vicious circle that is shattering American communities.

——

The folks I grew up with deserve better than the choices either party has offered in the past couple of elections. Liberals promise a big, intrusive, and all-providing government that sucks the life and faith out of families and communities.

But conservatives give the impression that they are unconcerned about the millions of hurting and vulnerable Americans. No wonder so many people stayed home on Election Day 2012. Our country needs opportunities for all, not just the financiers on the East Coast or the high-tech tycoons on the West. And that means focusing on what will strengthen the families and communities of ordinary Americans who want to work.

When I ran for president, I noticed that what stuck in people's minds was not my policy pronouncements but images (not the ones that political consultants contrive, but something as simple as a sweater vest) and stories like the one I told the night I won the Iowa caucuses. I recalled kneeling next to my grandfather's coffin, where all I could do was look at his hands. They were the powerful hands of a miner, thick and scarred. It struck me then that those hands dug freedom for me.

In the last few years, a lot of us have realized that we can lose that freedom. In fact, we may be perilously close to losing it right now. America should be a land of opportunity and its people full of hope. But I saw firsthand the hopelessness in the eyes of thousands of our countrymen. Who is going to help them? There are things we can do, but we'll need the resolve of heroes. This country, thank God, has never been short of heroes.

In the chapters to follow, I'll explore what went wrong and what killed opportunity for so many Americans. And I'll share my ideas about how we can rebuild this economy and our communities. If running for president teaches you anything, it's that no one has all the answers. But there's one thing I know with absolute certainty—we Americans have always met the challenges that history has thrown at us, and we can meet them again.

CHAPTER TWO

RESTORING THE AMERICAN DREAM FOR WORKERS

All of us have a picture in our head of what the American Dream looks like. It probably includes owning your own home, having a family and a good job, being active in your church and community, sending your kids off to college or technical school, and then retiring comfortably and spoiling your grandkids. Whatever variation each of us has of this vision, the American Dream is always the dream of a better life for us and for our children, of leaving our little corner of the world better than we found it.

If you ask people what trait is most characteristically American, many of them will answer "rugged individualism." It's true that this country's respect for the dignity and freedom of the individual is unique in the history of the world, and it's at the heart of America's success. From the beginning of our nation, we have believed our rights come from God, not from the state, and God bestows those rights one person at a time. But it's important to remember that the American Dream has never just been about the individual.

I part company with the libertarians here. They hold that the basic unit of society is the individual. That's wrong. The basic unit of society is the family. No one comes into this world as a self-sufficient individual. We start out as the helpless child of a mother and a father, who put aside their own desires and interests to care for us. The family, in fact, is the first society— the first government, the first classroom, the first church. And the strength of the family is the strength of "we."

I first learned the importance of "we" on my seventh-grade basketball team, and I've learned it over and over again bringing up seven children with Karen. No one ever raised a barn, cleared a forest, built a company, or won a war by himself. Call it teamwork, cooperation, fellowship, solidarity, or whatever you like—working with and serving others is the secret not only of success but of happiness.

Two and a half centuries of history have proved that the American Dream is real. Our dynamic free-market system built a ladder of wealth and opportunity that millions have climbed from poverty to prosperity. In America, you're not limited by who your parents were or which side of the tracks you were born on. What economists like to call "upward economic mobility" the rest of us just call the American Dream.

Ask an American what the keys to success are, and he'll tell you hard work, education, creativity, perseverance, and some good fortune. In Europe you get a very different answer. A recent survey found that many Europeans believe the keys to success are whom you know, what family you come from, and what connections you have in the government. That's the attitude you'll find in a country where government picks winners and losers. It's not capitalism but crony capitalism. In much of the world, of course, the corruption goes far deeper. Don't get me wrong—connections help in this country too, but in America there are too many people who have earned their success for us to be as cynical as people in other countries.[1]

We're at risk, though, of slipping into the same vicious economic cycles caused by cronyism that have plagued Europe. Our system is increasingly littered with bailouts, tax loopholes, and subsidies that corporations exploit using high-priced lobbyists. Unfortunately, cronyism has been the order of the day in the Obama administration. When big government arbitrarily decides how it will enforce the new healthcare laws and against whom, and when it rewards its favorite "green" industries with taxpayer subsidies, the demons of crony capitalism are set loose.

The cronyism is extending into the boardroom with politicians and corporate executives scratching each other's backs. Look at the maddening unfairness behind the "too big to fail" financial crises in 2008–2009. Although his bank was teetering on the brink of bankruptcy and complete failure, the chairman of Citigroup earned more than $126 million during his two-year tenure there, made possible by a bailout paid for by you, the taxpayer![2]

I'm a sports nut, and I like to compare capitalism to a football game. The competition is intense and the stakes are high. There are winners and losers, and everyone is in it to win. Capitalism, like the NFL, has a rulebook and officials who enforce those rules.

Some libertarian-leaning capitalists have become so frustrated with government that they want to eliminate federal agencies and officials responsible for enforcing the law. Every football fan complains about the officials, particularly when it seems like they are throwing flags on every other play, but without the refs there would be chaos. For example, a holding penalty could be called on every play, but it isn't. The officials generally call only penalties that affect the play. So if a left tackle holds on a wide receiver screen to the right, the official lets it go. Yes, rules are rules, but there is the larger picture to keep in mind—football succeeds when the players have an opportunity to perform at their best individually and as a team. The NFL knows that no one comes to the game to see officials perform. It wants them to avoid unnecessary calls that interfere with the game and to work with the players to keep this intense, violent sport from getting out of hand.

President Obama, by contrast, believes that the game of capitalism is fundamentally flawed. He directs his officials not only to call more penalties but to change the rules in the middle of the game to reflect what he thinks is "fair." Imagine a game in which the rules change depending on whom the commissioner is rooting for or in which officials call penalties on only one team. In some areas of the economy today, the government referees have not only swallowed their whistles, they've put on jerseys and joined one of the teams!

The American economy transformed human history because of freedom—free markets, free workers, free entre-preneurs. That freedom is endangered, and with it the American Dream.

———

The Declaration of Independence proclaims: "We hold these truths to be self-evident, that all men are created equal, that they are endowed by their Creator with certain unalienable Rights, that among these are Life, Liberty and the pursuit of Happiness." That's where the American Dream started. The term itself was coined by James Truslow Adams in 1931 in a book titled *The Epic of America*.[3] Writing at the onset of the Great Depression, he described that dream of a land in which life should be better and richer and fuller for everyone, with opportunity for each according to ability or achievement.

It is a difficult dream for the European upper classes to appreciate, and too many of us Americans have grown weary and mistrustful of it. It is not just a dream of motor cars and high wages, but a dream of a social order in which each person can develop his or her gifts and talents to the fullest degree and enjoy the recognition to which he or she is entitled, regardless of the accident of birth or position.

That's why I don't like to talk about the "middle class," a term favored, unfortunately, by politicians of both parties. I refuse to accept the premise of that term, "middle class." As conservatives, we don't believe there are social or economic classes in America. Unlike the Left, we believe in the dignity of every human life and seek to create a country that maximizes his or her God-given potential. We shouldn't assign people to categories or divide them artificially, pitting one group against another. That's a specialty of this president and the Left, and we should reject it by eliminating this divisive rhetoric from our lexicon.

Another reason I don't talk about the "middle class" is that the term has no real meaning in the United States. In a 2012 Pew Research survey, only 7 percent of respondents identified themselves as lower class, and 2 percent as upper class.[4] A wonderful characteristic of Americans is that almost everyone sees himself as the average person. Let's stick to a term that describes the people who are working and doing the best they can to be good citizens but are falling behind—working Americans.

=====

The American Dream is ingrained in us. It is the reason people risk their lives every day to come here. It is why parents scrimp and save to get their kids through college. Everyone knows the American Dream takes work—we take fewer days of vacation than almost any other people in the world—but many are willing to pay the price to reach their dream.[5]

Many Americans, however, are losing their grip on the dream. A Marist-McClatchy poll taken in February 2014 found that only 31 percent of Americans believe that someone who works hard has a good chance of improving his standard of living, while 68 percent think that someone who works hard has a difficult time even maintaining his standard of living. Eighty percent of Americans think it's harder now to get ahead than in previous generations, and 78 percent expect it to be even harder for the next generation.[6] Those numbers should be a punch in the gut to every American leader, starting with the president.

To put a face on these statistics about the American Dream, I'd like to introduce you to a family I'll call the Harrisons.

They are a composite of the many hundreds of families I met and the thousands of stories I collected during my campaign. James and Susan Harrison live in northeastern Ohio and have two teenage boys. A generation ago, the Harrisons' parents were relatively well-off, enjoying comfortable, happy lives. James's father worked for a company that manufactured aluminum tubes. It was a secure job with good wages. Susan grew up five blocks away, and her father was the football coach at the high school. James and Susan went to good public schools, participated in sports and the Key Club, and were faithful parishioners at their Roman Catholic church. James spent his high school summers working for the aluminum company and had a job waiting there for him when he graduated. He and Susan got married several years after that, and within a few years they had two boys. They never thought much about becoming rich in a material sense, but they saw a clear path to a life rich in family and community, coaching Little League and raising their children in a safe, hardworking neighborhood.

Life started pretty well for the Harrisons, but then things changed. Business at the aluminum company peaked about thirty years ago and has steadily declined ever since. James's wages flattened, and then his benefits started to get cut back. Ten years ago, the company filed for bankruptcy and everyone lost his job. Since then, James has worked at a big-box home improvement store thirty miles away. With fewer hours and no benefits, he is earning about three-quarters of his old wage and spending more money on gas for his commute.

Susan Harrison works part-time as a school nurse. Her hours have been cut back, and the family's finances are tight. Their kids are now in high school, but those once-proud public schools are a shadow of their former selves. The Little League continues on, but the fields are weedier and the rosters smaller.

The Harrisons feel they are too old for new training and education, and with teenage boys and elderly parents, they can't easily pick up and move. College for their kids looks unaffordable, and at the same time, they don't want the boys loading up on debt. They have little hope for a better future or to regain the pride and comfort their family once enjoyed. All around them they see neighbors slipping into poverty. They see drug and alcohol abuse and young girls getting pregnant without husbands, relying on the state for their welfare. Their once-safe neighborhood now has vacant homes and crime.

━━━━

What hope does our country offer the Harrisons? Is there still a path to prosperity for all Americans? After talking to people across the United States, my sense is that they want to believe in the American Dream, but it's getting harder. Too many shuttered factories and abandoned homes stand as ghostly reminders of the prosperity and stability that working Americans once enjoyed. Crime, despair, and social break-down have taken their place.

These are not sudden developments—many of these com-munities have been in decline for decades—but the Great Recession knocked away their last struts. Not only were eight million jobs lost, and more than half of all household wealth, but the local manufacturing plants and supporting businesses are not there anymore for young people starting their careers.

For the most part, people like the Harrisons have tradi-tional, conservative values; they believe in family and faith; they are willing to work hard; they are patriotic, with a patri-otism that ties them to their community. And what have we Republicans offered them? Mostly macroeconomic arguments about tax policies that won't affect them directly. The Harri-sons can be forgiven if they feel like Republicans have no idea what is happening to average Americans today.

Give President Obama credit—his campaign focused relentlessly on stories about people who were suffering, and he was able to convince most voters that he cared. He deem-phasized work as a path to prosperity by gutting the welfare reforms that were a bipartisan achievement of Bill Clinton's presidency, then he dramatically expanded relief programs with no work requirement—programs like food stamps, school lunches, and unemployment insurance. Burdened with an atrocious economic record, Obama's campaign developed an astonishingly effective strategy: let voters continue to blame

President Bush for the problems, wage a rhetorical war on the wealthy, emphasize the redistribution of wealth, and play on people's fear that "millionaires and billionaires" were trying to pull the rug out from under them.

That strategy succeeded in getting Obama reelected, but it has done nothing to improve the economy or help the people who are hurting. In 2008, Obama promised "hope and change." He delivered the change—above all, the disastrous and unpopular Obamacare—but hope was replaced in 2012 by fear. The people who supported Obama most strongly were those who felt economically vulnerable—ethnic minorities and single women. To be sure, the president made other appeals to this base (the shamefully divisive "war on women" comes to mind), but fear of losing the government safety net, even if you're not currently relying on it yourself, proved to be a decisive issue.

We have an obligation to deal with people's legitimate fear during this time of great hardship, change, and uncertainty. The answer to every problem can't be "Quit whining and buck up." (See how that would work in your marriage!) We must articulate a reassuring vision for those who are struggling, and it must focus on the importance of work and personal dignity.

━━━━━

The fear and anxiety bred by the weak economy and the breakdown of the family are bad enough, but lately they have given rise to a disturbingly un-American malady—hopelessness. The monthly unemployment report in this anemic recovery results in a partisan sparring match between Left and Right with both sides using statistics to bolster their political narratives. One number has been the most telling over the past five years—the percentage of people who have simply given up looking for work is at or near all-time highs.

People believe the American Dream is fading. It's no surprise that people are dissatisfied with our country's economic situation. But most people no longer expect things to get better. Indeed, in some ways—paying for college tuition, affording retirement, finding good jobs—they expect things to get worse. Are they wrong? Maybe not. Not only is our economy in a recession, but economic mobility is lagging behind many other countries.[7] According to a Brookings Institution report, you are about two times more likely to rise up the economic ladder in Canada or Australia than you are in America.[8]

The one area of the country where upward mobility is comparable to these countries is the place with the strongest families and an ethic of community support—the Salt Lake City area. Thanks to the Mormon Church, marriage and family are paramount there, and the church fosters an impressive network of private-sector relief for families in economic distress.

When social scientists study the ability of people to rise out of poverty, one of their findings is so consistent that it cannot be denied or ignored: children from two-parent families who live in communities where the two-parent family is the norm have a much higher chance of succeeding.[9] That doesn't mean there aren't thousands of heroic single mothers doing everything they can for their children. But our appreciation for those women must not distract us from the fact that, as a rule, children do better when their mom and dad are married and living at home.

———

Perhaps the most troubling news about the state of the American Dream is how we define success. A 2012 survey found that "fame and fortune" are replacing "faith and family" as the central components of the American Dream.[10] If the character of George Bailey in *It's a Wonderful Life* once embodied Americans' idea of true success, he has been replaced by the latest winner of *American Idol*. Yet the greatest reward in life is not becoming a rich celebrity; it is having a family—which happens to be a much more democratic ideal. Barbara Walters, who has been a cheerleader for liberalism for decades, has admitted that her greatest regret in life is that she didn't have more children.[11] Warren Buffett, one of the richest men in the world, also recognizes the hollowness of Hollywood ideals. When a student asked him how he defined success, the brilliant investor dismissed almost out of hand his fame and financial achievements and said what matters most is "whether the people you care about most love you."[12]

It may be that many young people are turning their backs on the traditional American Dream in part because it seems unattainable. They make up what economists are calling a "lost generation"—millions of twenty-something college graduates who are deep in student debt, can't find a good job, and might never get a foot on the ladder of career, family, and homeownership. As many as six and a half million Americans between the ages of sixteen and twenty-four are neither in school nor in the workforce.[13] They may never recover, and their children will face even gloomier prospects.

Bigger and fatter federal entitlement programs will not bring hope to the Harrisons and their children. They don't want food stamps. They want the dignity of a decent job and a fair shot at a better life for their kids. Hope lies in a vision of families and communities in which human beings thrive, and in policies based on that vision. I'll have more to say later about incentives for manufacturers and small businesses, a tax system that encourages marriage and strong families, and education that is affordable and practical.

In the meantime, the Ohio town where the Harrison family lives sits on the Utica Shale, which promises well-paying jobs in the oil and gas industry for James and his sons and thousands of others. There are also powerful political forces that want to strangle that industry, and they have the sympathetic ear of the president and his party. Yet Republicans have somehow ended up as the bad guys in this story. I'm going to show you in this book how we can change that.

———

Ultimately, the American Dream has never really been about the dreamer. My grandfather, like millions of others, came to America seeking a better life. But the better life he was after was for his children. In this exceptional country, he was able to nourish in his children the values of faith, family, work, freedom, service, and patriotism. He prospered here, and I thank God for the economic blessings. But my grandfather built something more important than wealth. He built a family, a spiritual legacy, and he built it to last. Over a million immigrants a year come to this country in search of the same dream, because they still believe that dream is within their grasp.

We need to remember, as we debate about policies and fight our political battles, what's really at stake. The American Dream is about a country of prosperous communities, strong families, a decent life today, and a realistic hope for a better tomorrow. Blue collar conservatives understand that, and it's time Republicans let them know that we do too.

CHAPTER THREE

A GOP THAT STANDS UP FOR EVERYONE

Americans are more pessimistic than ever. Washington is a mess. The economy has been sputtering along for years. The culture is getting even coarser. It is harder to find a good job, much less climb the ladder of success. For a working young man or woman who wants to raise a family, the search for a good spouse feels like finding a needle in a haystack, and the odds against a lasting marriage are sobering.

Though some of today's problems are new, Americans have faced serious challenges before, and we have always prevailed.

Sometimes in the hour of crisis, we have been blessed with a great leader. Abraham Lincoln guided us through the Civil War. Franklin Roosevelt inspired us with the determination to defeat Nazism and fascism in World War II. Ronald Reagan restored our confidence after the economic, military, and political crises of the 1970s and led us to victory in the Cold War.

There is no such leader in the Oval Office now, no one who can appeal to the values that make this country great because he believes in them himself. President Obama doesn't understand America. Maybe that's because he was raised in a radical family, much of the time overseas, and educated by people who saw only the worst in this country. He abandoned the slogan of "hope" a long time ago. When Obama appeals to Americans, his themes are envy, resentment, and fear. He can mobilize his base on the Left with that talk, but it falls flat with everyone else.

Borrowing a page from the unhappier chapters of European history, Obama promises that the government will take care of every want and need. All the public has to do is cede control of their lives to the benevolent functionaries of the omnicompetent state. Uttering the world's stalest political pickup line, he woos an anxious electorate: "Trust me, your leader, with more power and control because I really do care for you, and of course I know what is best." In tough times, people who feel economically vulnerable—the poor, minorities, and single women—have decided to stay with their date.

For Obama, there's no such thing as the "loyal opposition," only the enemy that must be identified and "punished." Call them conservatives, Tea Partiers, libertarians, or the religious Right, this president has them in his crosshairs in virtually every speech he gives. And his administration doesn't shrink from using the coercive power of the federal government to make the point.

Americans are beginning to see how brutally the Democrats are willing to exercise their power, whether it's the use of the Internal Revenue Service to harass political opponents, the subversion of the Senate filibuster as a check on majoritarian tyranny, or the abuse of executive orders to thwart the constitutional role of Congress. Yet as scandal follows scandal, Republicans fail to persuade the American people that they are more trustworthy than the Democrats, and the federal government settles deeper into dysfunction.

Americans have had it, and they want real leadership that understands them and what it will take to get America going again.

———

All they got from the election of 2012 was a clinic in the divide-and-conquer politics of the Left. President Obama was reelected because he rallied his base of minorities, single women, and youth by painting a picture of Mitt Romney as a heartless rich guy who had made millions by putting everyday Americans out of work. That coalition might not seem big enough to win a national election, and if this were 1980 that would be true. Had Romney received the same percentage of the vote of every ethnic group that Ronald Reagan received in 1980 (when the Gipper carried forty-eight states against Jimmy Carter), Romney probably would have suffered an even bigger loss to Obama.

The Democrats are masters of demography, and with the eager help of the media they bombard the public with the message of the Republican war against women, the young, the poor, and immigrants. Republicans, they say, represent only the rich; they don't care about the folks trying to climb out of poverty. So far, it has worked—in spite of a miserable economy that hurts those very groups more than any other, the Democrats have managed to solidify their base.

This message is ceaseless, overhyped, and cynical, but is any of it true? Let's hit the hanging curve ball first. Do Republicans really care less about the person at the bottom of the ladder than Democrats do? To be painfully honest, I would have to say in some ways "yes." There are some in my party who have taken the ideal of individualism to such an extreme that they have forgotten the obligation to look out for our fellow man. The rhetoric is often harsh and gives the all-too-willing media an opportunity to tar all Republicans with the same brush. That is not my Republican Party. In fact, in 2005 I wrote a book titled *It Takes a Family: Conservatism and the Common Good*. We must not cede the moral high ground on promoting the common good or the issue of caring for the less fortunate to a party whose own misguided policies have trapped so many in a life of poverty and despair.

We Republicans have neglected to focus our policies and our rhetoric on the plight of lower-income Americans. For thirty years our theme has been that the Reagan tax cuts transformed the American economy and further tax cuts will make it even better. While I believe that's true, our critics on the Left have a couple of valid points.

First, when Reagan cut rates in the early 1980s, the top rate was 70 percent; today it is slightly under 40 percent.[1] The impact on the economy of further cuts will therefore not be as dramatic. At the same time, the drag on the economy of the current rate of taxation is not as severe as it was in 1980. Reagan's economic policy responded to the problems confronting America at the time: high inflation and stagnant growth—a toxic mix we called "stagflation." Growth is anemic today not primarily because of high individual tax rates but because of excessive government regulation of businesses. Our focus on tax cuts for individuals not only leaves us open to the "tax breaks for the rich" sloganeering of the Left but seems irrelevant to the nearly 50 percent of the population who don't pay federal income taxes today.

The second point that we need to address is that while the technological revolution has increased the material wealth of our society as a whole and improved the quality of life for all

Americans, it has also left our society more polarized. The new economy bestows a larger share of its rewards on the educated than the industrial economy did.

Ronald Reagan offered a remedy for what ailed America in 1980. He would be the last person to offer exactly the same prescription more than three decades later under quite different circumstances. We need a different game plan to achieve economic growth with an eye toward those whom the new economy has left behind. If we only promise more growth without addressing the 70 percent of young Americans who will not earn a bachelor's degree, we will be shirking our responsibility to them and handing the Democrats an electoral club to beat us with.[2]

So our critics are right—the American economy has changed dramatically since 1980, and our policies must reflect that change. But something else has changed as well—the American household—and it's liberals who ignore this change. In 1980, 55 percent of black children were born out of wedlock, and the out-of-wedlock birth rate in the population as a whole was 18 percent. Today, almost three out of four black children are born without a father in the home, and over 40 percent of all American children will grow up fatherless.[3] Democrats can talk all day long about the "War on Poverty," but the most effective antipoverty tool is a combination of work, education, and marriage. America created the new economy, but a fatherless America cannot produce the skilled and functional workers, particularly men, who will thrive in that economy. The liberal programs of the last fifty years are no solution to the problem of family breakdown, and neither are tax cuts. The severity of this problem grows exponentially with each new generation. If we don't address it now, it won't be long before our economy reaches the "do not resuscitate" stage.

———

Republicans need to remember the old adage that "people don't care what you know until they know that you care."

After losing the election, Mitt Romney acknowledged the party's problem. Talking to a reporter while volunteering at a homeless shelter, he remarked that the men and women there "are used to being ignored, I guess. Mostly by people like me."[4]

I admire his willingness to shoulder some of the responsibility for the problem, but as a matter of fact, Romney has a splendid record of helping people in all walks of life. A leader in his church, he has been fully engaged in its philanthropic efforts over the years. As an employer, he showed his concern for even the most junior employee, and he has given millions of dollars to help those who are less fortunate. Mitt Romney is a model of compassion for those less fortunate than himself, but how many people know about it? He has lived the American Dream not only by succeeding in business and raising a beautiful family but also—and just as importantly—by serving those in need.

It should come as no surprise that Americans are the most generous people in the world. Study after study shows that

Americans give more than anyone else to help their fellow man. We rank number one in the annual World Giving Index.[5] In 2013, Germany ranked twenty-second, India ninety-third, and China came in next to last, ahead of only bankrupt Greece. But what about American conservatives? Surely they are stingier with the poor than their liberal neighbors.

Arthur Brooks, the president of the American Enterprise Institute, has studied how America's giving breaks down by political ideology and other factors, and he finds that conservatives, especially religious conservatives, are actually the most generous with their own money. Liberals are terribly generous, too—with other people's money. To be fair, religious liberals (those who attend church once a week or more) are also quite generous, but there aren't many of them.[6]

Compare the charitable giving of Mitt Romney, a well-to-do empty nester, to the other wealthy empty nester on the national ticket, Joe Biden. Romney gave 29 percent of his money to charity in the past few years, whereas Joe Biden gave only 0.5 percent.[7] But Romney is the uncaring, wealthy Scrooge, and Biden the common, compassionate Bob Cratchit simply because Biden wants to use the force of the government to take even more money away from high earners and give it to those he chooses. The liberal media promote this as caring, but it's not. It is not about giving and helping, it is about power, and it doesn't reflect the true spirit of America.

If conservatives are so generous, why does the GOP have the reputation as the party of Scrooge? It might be because we spend so much time talking to and about the "job creator" and business owner. Economic growth and the role of the job creator should continue to be at the heart of our economic policy, but we need to think about, listen to, and talk about the *jobholder* as well. If conservatives got the vote of every job creator in the country, we'd still lose. We must earn a large portion of the votes of jobholders, because there are far more of them.

Two incidents from the 2012 campaign illustrate this truth. When President Obama told an audience of business owners, "You didn't build that," he appeared to denigrate the role of entrepreneurship in the economy, and Republicans thought he had made a disastrous misstep. We even made it the theme of our national convention. The president's statement was revealing and galling, but it didn't matter. What percentage of Americans have built a business? The disastrous misstep of the campaign turned out to be Governor Romney's surreptitiously recorded comment about the "47 percent" of the population that collects payments from the government. It's basic math that you can't insult half of the voters and expect to win.

━━━━━

The Republican Party hasn't always had this problem with those who are trying to rise in America. We have an impressive history of speaking for all Americans, and we can reach them again. From its birth, our party was on the side of the struggling, for it was formed to combat slavery. The 1856 platform pledged to abolish the barbarism of slavery. Under the leadership of the first Republican president, Abraham Lincoln, it was. When Democrats attempted to derail the 1964 Civil Rights Act, Republicans helped push it through with the support of over 80 percent of their members.[8]

The party that now supposedly wages a "war on women" led the fight for women's right to vote. The first vote in Congress on women's suffrage occurred in 1878 on a constitutional amendment offered by a Republican, A. A. Sargent. A Democratic majority defeated it. It would be over thirty years before another vote was taken, and it was not until after the Republican landslide of 1918 that the Nineteenth Amendment, sponsored by another Republican, was taken up and passed.[9]

One of the greatest champions of the working man ever to occupy the White House was the "trust buster" Theodore Roosevelt, who took on corporate monopolies and pushed for landmark reforms of working conditions.

In recent years, Republicans have led the way on welfare reform, the Medicare prescription drug benefit, and educational initiatives like charter schools and vouchers (opportunities that Democrats have fought ferociously to deny to children from poor families). We have created tax policies to help create jobs in urban areas, lowered taxes, and put money back in the pockets of families. And, of course, we have always stood for marriage and responsible fatherhood. We rarely get credit for that record, in part because we don't bother to talk much about it.

———

Like the Democrats, today's Republican Party is a coalition of different interests, each with its own priorities. Those interests include Tea Party constitutionalists, small and medium-sized business owners, believers in the free market, those in favor of a strong defense and tough foreign policy, and social conservatives who put faith, family, and protecting the innocent and unborn first. We have our disagreements and vigorous debates, and we'll have them again in 2016, but we're all under the "big tent" of the GOP, and we respect and help each other.

I believe that in recent years, the interests of the "talk only about deficits and growth" wing of the party have received too much emphasis, and it has come at the expense of working families. Our party's "you built that" convention in 2012 didn't have much to say about the struggles of our working families. We weren't speaking to them. It hasn't just been our rhetoric—we have lacked ideas and policies. People like the Harrisons can't be blamed if they thought we Republicans "didn't care," and the media were happy to support this narrative.

Broadening our party's message will involve many political challenges, but everyone in our "big tent" wants a country where people have an opportunity to achieve the American

Dream: "Life, liberty, and the pursuit of happiness." We believe that now it's time to say and *do* something about it.

CHAPTER FOUR

HOLES IN THE BOAT

S ince Ronald Reagan came to Washington and launched the supply-side revolution, Republican economic policy could be expressed in one word—growth. "A rising tide lifts all boats," as we like to say, quoting that earlier tax cutter John F. Kennedy.[1] The theory is that by helping those at the top—the people who start businesses and create jobs—we help those at the bottom.

Our economic policy, therefore, has focused on tax cuts, deregulation, and free trade. While there have been a variety of different plans, from the "Fair Tax" to the "Flat Tax" to

"9-9-9," they were all aimed at lowering taxes on job creators to stimulate economic growth.[2] After more than thirty years of this policy, I think it is time Republicans ask themselves, "Does this really work?" The short answer is "Yes, but ..." The "yes" part is pretty clear. If government policies encourage growth and business owners and investors earn more profit ("the rising tide" part), businesses will grow, and there will be more jobs at higher wages ("lifting all boats"). Since the Reagan Revolution, America has had the strongest, most stable economy in the world thanks to economic freedom, relatively low taxes (with the notable exception of the federal corporate income tax), and, until recently, a reasonable regulatory and legal environment.[3] So why did I say the answer to the question "Does this work?" is "Yes, *but* ..."? Advances in technology have helped people even at the lowest income levels. Telecommunications and medical treatment, for example, are better for everyone than they were fifty years ago. But the income gap is widening, and for the 70 percent of Americans who won't get a college degree, it is increasingly difficult to find stable, full-time employment at wages that can support a family.[4] Republicans love to quote Ronald Reagan, who declared in his first inaugural address that "government is not the solution to our problem; government *is* the problem."[5] But you rarely hear the four words that preceded that line: "In this present crisis...." The economic crisis of our day is different from the one Reagan confronted in 1981. Everyone was struggling then—businesses, investors, and workers alike. Today, large businesses are doing well, and stock and commodity prices are strong. If you are an owner or investor, life has been pretty good. But for workers, it's a different story: unemployment and underemployment are high, and the percentage of working-age Americans who have given up looking for a job is at thirty-year highs.[6] In short, the well-educated, the business owner, and the investor from a stable family are doing fine, but millions of Americans who can't check those boxes are floundering. In an increasingly service-oriented economy, they are working part-time or in jobs that provide little prospect for advancement. The tide is rising, but many boats have holes of various sizes—for example, a lack of skills or experience, an unstable family, or no high school degree. They are sinking or are stuck on a sand bar. Lower-wage workers see the rich getting richer, but they feel poorer. Democrats are fond of saying that all the Republican talk about a "rising tide" really amounts to "trickle-down economics." That accusation may be shortsighted and not entirely fair, but we have to admit that for the people at the bottom, that's what it feels like these days—just a trickle.

———

President Obama recognizes the problem of sinking boats, but his answer, predictably, has been to raise taxes on those who are succeeding, borrow even more money, and hand out that money not only to people in sinking boats but to almost half the population.

So how has that worked out?

Here are the facts of the first four years of President Obama's attempt to tax and redistribute our way out of the wealth gap that existed when he took office. Income inequality has increased under President Obama.[7] The gap between the rich and the poor is wider than it has ever been in American history.[8] In President Obama's first term, the income of the top 1 percent grew 31.4 percent, while the income for everyone else grew just 0.4 percent.[9] Yes, you read that right— *less* than 1 percent. And the top 10 percent of all Americans now have 50 percent of all the wealth in this country.[10] Since the Great Recession ended, 95 percent of the gains have gone to just 1 percent of Americans.[11] It turns out that Obama's attempted Robin Hood act has actually helped the rich and hurt the poor.

Why hasn't taking from the rich benefited the poor? Higher taxes make America less competitive in the global economy for both jobs and investment capital. In spite of the Federal Reserve's desperate effort to counteract the administration's anti-growth policies by printing money, the economy continues to sputter. Slower growth hurts everyone, but it hurts marginal workers and low-wage workers more.

But how does a government handout hurt the recipient? How does it put more holes in the boats of people who are already sinking? The government programs that have expanded most under this stagnant economy are benefits to able-bodied people. These benefits carry no expectation of work, service, or repayment, and they create a disincentive to climb the ladder of success and happiness. When the Congressional Budget Office forecast that the most recent entitlement aimed at working Americans, Obamacare, would result in 2.5 million Americans choosing not to work, President Obama responded with a "mission-accomplished" thumbs up.

Providing health benefits is not the first disincentive to work the Left has promoted. Look at unemployment benefits as an example. Early in the recession, President Obama requested that unemployment benefits be extended to ninety-nine weeks.[12] At a time when the unemployment rate was over 10 percent, this was seen as an act of compassion.[13] But the purpose of unemployment insurance is to enable recipients to focus on getting a job, not to make it easier for them to stay out of work. Since the government began tracking long-term unemployment in the 1940s, no more than 25 percent of the unemployed had ever been out of work more than twenty-seven weeks,[14] and unemployment benefits usually lasted twenty-six weeks.[15] In 2010, by contrast, an unprecedented 47 percent of those on unemployment benefits received them for between six months and two years.

The longer someone receives unemployment benefits, the more difficult it becomes for him to return to employment.[16]

Consider how an employer is likely to view an able-bodied worker who has been on benefits for two years and, now that those benefits are exhausted, is applying for a job that is a step down from his previous position. The applicant's job skills have probably eroded, his work habits and attitude are questionable, and he is more likely than someone else to go back on unemployment. A long stay on unemployment makes the recipient less employable, which makes him less likely to be successful, independent, and happy. The politically popular extension of unemployment benefits, therefore, is less compassionate than it seems.

———

As my grandfather and dad drilled into me, hard work is the key to success and happiness. How tragic, then, that our government, which should promote the common good, undermines the work ethic of its citizens in so many ways. Even state-run gambling and lotteries promote the idea of get rich quick without earning it, instead of the slow and steady climb up the ladder that comes from working hard and improving your skills. An estimated 70 percent of lottery winners, who struck it rich, go broke.[17]

But more harm is done by welfare programs. The government "safety net," as the metaphor implies, is intended to catch us as we fall and help us bounce back to a position of safety and stability, ready to continue life's climb. It has evolved, unfortunately, into a hunter's net that ensnares the vulnerable, robbing them of their dignity and trapping them in generational poverty and hopelessness.

Designed with the best intentions, welfare programs, like Obamacare, have a "phaseout" feature. The more you (or your spouse) earn, the less you receive in government benefits. At first glance, phaseouts seem to make sense, but they are a powerful disincentive to take a job or get married. In other words, they discourage the behavior most necessary for rising out of poverty.

Glenn Grothman is a state senator in Wisconsin whom I met while campaigning there in 2012. He shared with me the startling fact that in his state, a single mother with two children was eligible for over $38,000 in a variety of government benefits as long as her income didn't exceed $15,000 a year. For every dollar she earned over that amount, she lost more than a dollar in benefits! If she married the man she was living with, he would have to earn over $60,000 a year for her to remain in the same place economically. In their desire to help, the architects of the welfare state have steered single mothers away from working and marrying. Millions of Americans face enough barriers to success—a poor education, poor work habits, a criminal record, lack of experience—without the government adding more.[18]

As more citizens receive government welfare benefits, the stigma is being replaced by an expectation of being on welfare, especially in areas where out-of-wedlock births are a multi-generational norm and government has replaced fathers. Without the stigma, recipients lose the sense of welfare as a temporary solution and see it simply as a way of life. When most of your neighbors live this way, there is no shame in living this way too. Programs designed to help in the short term do great harm in the long term.

Let me be clear: conservatives should not rail against properly incentivized government safety net programs for those whose lives have taken a bad turn, nor against government programs that provide lifesaving care for the disabled, the chronically ill, and the elderly. A compassionate and caring society should have such programs in place, but the programs must be private-public partnerships that are more affordable, more efficient, and better targeted than the current slate of programs.

With hopelessness and a lack of ambition comes crime—and not all of it happens out on the streets. When most of your neighbors live on the dole and accept it as a way of life, when you think of government benefits as something you deserve rather than something you tap only in an emergency, then it's a short step to figuring out a "creative" way to get at those benefits. This little act of fraud can go beyond stealing from the taxpayer to stealing from a community's own future. In a remarkable and heartbreaking column in the liberal *New York Times* last year, Nicholas Kristof described a poor rural community in Kentucky where parents admitted to taking their children out of literacy classes to protect a Supplemental Security Income benefit they received for having a "disabled" child.[19]

An entire legal subspecialty has developed around the aggressive pursuit of Social Security disability claims ("We don't take no for an answer!" one lawyer advertises). Fraud is far more widespread than you might imagine.[20] In some small, low-income towns, the retail stores are packed on the days disability checks are issued.

It's sad that people are in this position. It's sad that misguided government policy has made it worse. And it's sad that the president hasn't learned anything from experience. It wasn't that long ago, in the 1990s, when I lead Republicans working with President Clinton to reform welfare in a way that preserved the safety net but got people back to work. Maybe it was tough love, but it was compassionate. Our goal was to encourage people to return to the labor force, enhance their job skills, and accept the responsibility (and earn the self-respect) that comes with employment. You need three things to avoid poverty—education, work, and marriage— and we tried to shore up all three. We ended welfare as an entitlement; we provided block grants to the states so that they could use the money in the most effective way, which included providing vocational training; and we strengthened enforcement of child support payments, among other provisions.

Welfare rolls plummeted, poverty rates fell, people went back to work, and we showed that while poverty is an undeniable problem, it need not be an inescapable condition.

The Clinton-era welfare reform would seem to be a bipartisan success story. But the Obama administration has reversed much of that achievement, particularly the work requirements[21]—a bad deal for taxpayers and for the welfare recipients themselves. The best welfare programs are transitional welfare programs, programs that provide incentives and opportunities to work.

Social Security and Medicare, which have essentially eliminated poverty among vulnerable seniors and the disabled, show that government has an important role. But the best welfare provider is not government, whose bureaucrats see bloated caseloads as justification for bigger budgets. No, the best welfare program is individuals, families, and communities helping each other.

━━━

Perverse incentives are by no means limited to welfare programs. When I was in Congress, we went after the cozy relationships in the boardrooms of public corporations that resulted in rich rewards for mediocre and even failed executive teams. Executives were often rewarded when they produced short-term shareholder gains at the expense of the long-term health of the enterprise. I had the privilege of serving on the board of directors of a Fortune 500 company for five years after I left the Senate, and I saw for myself how these measures changed behavior in the boardroom. The regulations weren't perfect—they were burdensome, costly, and in many areas ineffective—but the attention curbed some of the outrageous abuses when directors were publicly reminded that their duty is to shareholders, and dare I say employees, not the corporate brass.

Nevertheless, the culture of many large companies still encourages a short-term outlook and disproportionate rewards for executives at the expense of shareholders and workers. Business leaders are more richly rewarded in America than in almost any other country, and it's hard to believe that *that* many of them are *that* good.

Welfare cheats aren't the only ones who would benefit from a little stigma. A free economic order, like a free political order, requires a certain level of integrity throughout the system. The government can't police every corporate act. The system relies on the honor and integrity of its participants—investors, directors, executives, and ordinary employees. The short-term, quick-buck mentality and the loose ethics that result from a materialistic "just do it" culture encourage investor scams and corporate malfeasance. Are the wolves of Wall Street responsible for welfare fraud? Yes, in part. In every civilization the elites have always set an example for the rest of society. When the average American sees that the result of systemic corruption is billions of dollars in Wall Street bailouts of the banks that caused the financial meltdown and the resulting Great Recession, with only a handful of prosecutions, the message is delivered. This is what Pope Francis was referring to in his critique of "trickle-down" capitalism that is practiced in his native South America. Crony capitalism and corruption undermine the trust that is necessary for a free economy to create jobs and economic security.

———

The growing disparity between rich and poor is part of a broader trend we might call cultural Balkanization. Americans increasingly associate with people of like mind and like income. In the news we follow, the entertainment we consume, the churches we worship in, and the neighborhoods we live in, we tend to see and hear people a lot like ourselves.[22] In the cities and towns of our country, there were always two sides of the tracks. You came from one side or the other, but you were separated from the people on the other side by a railroad track, not a gated community twenty miles from the other neighborhood. We long ago lost the village where rich and poor lived within walking distance of each other. Now we are separated not just by zoning and planned developments but by fear and envy.

People in a Balkanized society don't understand each other and don't have empathy for each other. In the America I grew up in, the union worker and the lawyer attended the same church, ate at the same restaurants, went to the same doctor and dentist, golfed at the same public course, read the same newspaper, drank Iron City beer, and watched *M*A*S*H* and the evening news with either Walter Cronkite or David Brinkley.

Now the wealthy worship in a superparish or megachurch in the suburbs as the old city churches crumble. How many average-income, working Americans do you see at fancy restaurants or country clubs? Do you read the *Wall Street Journal* or the *New York Times* or just the local paper? Can you afford the craft beers, or do you have a Bud? Do you watch Hallmark or HBO? MSNBC or Fox News? Sure, there were choices in the past, but we are far more segmented now. Many of the divisions are determined by wealth, and that isn't a good thing.

Recently, I debated Howard Dean at Northwestern University. We were asked what America's greatest virtue is. He answered, "Diversity." Diversity can be good or bad, but it's not necessarily a virtue for society; it is, in fact, a challenge. "E pluribus unum," the motto the Founding Fathers chose for their new nation, expresses something essential for its survival. "Out of many, one"—the United States was a joint venture undertaken by a people representing varied backgrounds. The role of any government is to fashion laws that help us get along with each other so we can reach our full potential—our American Dream.

In America today, the economic elite are clustered in places like Manhattan, Boston, the suburbs north of Chicago, the Bay Area, pockets of Southern California, and Northwest Washington, D.C. These are the places where people who funded the campaigns of both President Obama and Governor Romney live. The people there shop at Whole Foods, listen to National Public Radio, and read the *New Yorker*. If they drink beer, it's imported or micro-brewed. They may follow the local professional sports franchises, but they're just as likely to spend their time doing yoga or collecting wine. They are more likely to spend Sunday morning at Starbucks than at church. Their children will have every possible advantage—good schools, the best healthcare, safe neighborhoods, lots of activities, and exposure to many role models and good examples.[23]

Most of America doesn't live like this, of course. Most of America shops at Sam's Club, drinks Coors, likes to hunt or fish, and goes to church or the American Legion. In his important book *Coming Apart: The State of White America, 1960–2010*, Charles Murray details the economic and social distress of blue collar Americans at a time when elites are prospering as never before. You'll find Murray's "New Upper Class" in places like "Belmont," the fictional town that represents the suburban enclaves of the wealthy and highly educated. The "New Lower Class" reside in neighborhoods represented by "Fishtown," the deteriorating home of people with no college degree who are sliding down the economic ladder. In Belmont, says Murray, the work ethic, families, and community spirit have held up or even improved over the years. In Fishtown they're all weaker, and the town is caught in a downward spiral. The social problems that result from deteriorating communities—teenage pregnancy, substance abuse, incarceration—get worse with each new generation. If you're born to a poor single mother who has dropped out of school, the odds are enormously stacked against you.

People like James and Susan Harrison live in Fishtown, of course. The once-proud community of Italian, Polish, and black families has deteriorated with its citizens' work ethic. They seem to have lost what it takes to hold together a hardworking but secure life. The decline starts with the loss of a job, followed by the inability to send their kids to college, divorce, out-of-wedlock pregnancy, single-mother households, food stamps, and a new generation of children with little potential to achieve anything.

———

The experience of the Harrisons has been studied in depth, and we know what predicts whether someone will live in poverty. During my campaign for president, I often cited a study from the Brookings Institution, a center-left think tank, which found that if you do these three things, it's very unlikely that you'll end up in poverty: graduate from high school, get a full-time job, and wait until you are married to have children. Only 8 percent of the people who do all three end up in poverty.[24] And those who don't do all three? Seventy-nine percent of them are poor sooner or later. That's a pretty startling statistic, right? Graduate, get a job, and wait until you're married to have kids. That's pretty much what separates the rich from the poor in our country.

But too many kids in communities that have suffered economically are failing to take those basic steps, in part because of a culture that promotes premarital sex and a president whose biggest campaign issue was free contraception to everyone, particularly unmarried young girls. Children of teenage mothers are much more likely to slip into the behavior that keeps them from graduating from high school, holding a job, and getting married. And on and on and on it goes. It's heartbreaking, yet the president and his party, who will do nothing about the crisis themselves, denounce any attempt to address it as a "war on women."

———

The real Fishtowns—the faded communities across America like my hometown of Butler, Pennsylvania—have lost jobs because of foreign competition and offshore labor, bad corporate and union leadership, and neglectful elected officials. To make ends meet, the people in those towns have been left to retail and service-sector jobs that offer fewer hours and no benefits. Or they rely on public assistance, in some cases becoming permanently dependent.

Since 2009, 14.7 million people have been added to the food stamp rolls, while only a few hundred thousand net new jobs have been created. The staggering fact is that we have added seventy-five new food stamp recipients for every new job.[25] And the burden on taxpayers to fund this expansion of welfare is growing dangerously.

The Harrisons don't want what the Democrats are offering—a handout. But they also don't want to hear about prosperity "trickling down" to them—they see that as an excuse to keep the status quo. They are fed up with both approaches and don't care to hear much from their elected leaders anymore.

What the Harrisons want are commonsense ideas that generate economic activity and opportunities that will help restore the proud town they grew up in. They aren't moving, because they feel there is still enough community, enough connection to the past, for their town to rise again if given a chance. They are optimistic about a new industry emerging to extract the natural gas from the shale rock deep underneath their town. They hope it will create opportunity for them and their kids.

The Harrisons want leaders who understand that their misfortune wasn't the result of laziness or bad life decisions. They were good employees, good parents, and good neighbors.

They are waiting for someone in Washington to understand, lay out a plan, and fight ... and it can't happen soon enough.

In the chapters that follow, I will outline what we can do for the millions of people like the Harrisons. There is hope— the American Dream is dying but not dead. We'll explore plans not for the rich or poor but for creating something for all of America to get excited about.

CHAPTER FIVE

RENEWING THE PURSUIT OF HAPPINESS

D uring the presidential campaign of 2012, Susan and James Harrison were inundated with phone calls, knocks on the door, and mailings. Living in Ohio and not clearly aligned with either party, they were targeted as swing voters in a battleground state. The Harrisons could not have avoided the candidates and the issues if they had wanted to.

But after all of that, the Harrisons ended up sitting out the election. They simply saw no reason to vote. James put in a long day on the store floor because he needed the extra pay.

Neither candidate offered them the hope of new opportunities.

On the one side, they saw a president seeking reelection after four miserable years. The economy was still in the tank, but Barack Obama was always attacking businesses. Too many of the neighbors had been laid off, and the Harrisons kept hearing about despair across the country. They knew about Obama's opposition to the Keystone pipeline, and they suspected he would fight the shale gas development that could help Ohio. They always attend church and believe in traditional marriage and in the sanctity of human life. Obama's views on these issues seemed so extreme, and that troubled them.

Governor Romney, on the other hand, never connected with them in a way that earned their confidence. When the Harrisons heard Romney's comment about the "47 percent," they took offense. The people he accused of "not contributing" sounded a lot like the people who lived on Social Security, military veterans, and other hardworking people who from time to time needed help. These people weren't moochers. They just needed an opportunity, and they didn't deserve the put-down.

You shouldn't think James and Susan are apathetic just because they didn't vote in 2012. They have always taken an interest in politics and discussed issues and candidates with their neighbors—especially at a time when so many people they knew were victims of the lousy economy. They have also been involved in civic affairs, their children's schools, and community groups. They are engaged Americans—and they are willing to engage even more if it will help them, their kids, and their friends and neighbors. But they want to know that their engagement is worthwhile.

The Harrisons weren't the only ones to feel left out in the 2012 election. In their home state of Ohio, for example, voter turnout in rural and traditionally blue collar counties was lower than in previous elections, including the Obama-McCain race in 2008.[1]

———

America's experience in the election of 2012 confirms what the book of Proverbs says, "Where there is no vision, the people perish."[2] Americans are desperate for leaders with vision—not number crunchers, not technocrats, not policy wonks, but men and women who can look beyond this week's polls and next year's election, who see clearly where we need to be headed. A lot of people thought they had found that leader in 2008, but Barack Obama's vision of an America "transformed" has been a nightmare, especially for those struggling hardest.

If you are born into poverty or are going through hard times, wouldn't you be better off if you were surrounded by institutions like churches, good schools, scouts, and strong families? We need stronger marriages, stronger churches, and stronger communities because they do what the government cannot do. Yet the liberal establishment that controls our government, our schools, the media, and so many of the institutions that shape our public life and form our opinions is busy tearing down these pillars of American society, starting with the family.

Government has taken the lead in liberating men from the responsibility of providing and caring for their children and their children's mother by providing single mothers with an alternative to building a relationship with the father of their child. Let's face it, government welfare benefits have played a role in the demise of marriage in low-income communities and have encouraged a new cultural norm that leads to multigenerational poverty and hopelessness.[3] Believe it or not, that's exactly what President Obama and his friends on the Left have in mind. It is their radical, anti-family dogma that government is the liberator of women and a suitable replacement for unfit fathers.

When I make this point in town hall meetings, someone usually objects that a mother and her child are better off without a convicted felon, gang member, dropout, unemployable dad in the picture. Fair enough, but to that child, as broken as her father may be, he is still her daddy, and she wants his love. What child doesn't want that? And how do you think the dad ended up like that? Almost 85 percent of young men in prison grew up without a father in their home.[4] Without dads in their lives, young men are much more likely to join a gang, drop out of school, father a child out of wedlock, abandon that child and the child's mother, and fail to hold down a decent job. Not having a father in the home hurts all children, but especially boys.

President Obama does not inflict on his own family the ruinous fantasy that a check from the government is as good as a father. I'm sure he's a caring and loving father because he knows how much it means to his children. Let's stop inflicting that fantasy on the poor, whose lives it devastates most.

The Left may have invented the welfare system that robs low-income children of their birthright and destroys their best chance to climb out of poverty, but with the exception of the 1996 Welfare Reform Act, the Right has done little to repair it. I know, because I worked on this issue in the conservative world for the better part of twenty years, and it was a pretty lonely fight. There are a few scholars at conservative think tanks who write about this problem and a handful of congressmen who try to tackle it, but few conservatives in public life work on policies aimed at the working poor.

It's not that conservatives don't care. Most of them support transforming the social welfare system. But it's a very low priority, so conservatives are complicit in allowing the destructive status quo to persist. For the good of our party and, above all, the good of our country, we must dismantle and replace the failed system we have now. What would a conservative alternative look like?

——

In 1776, when the American Dream was born, the average life expectancy in this country was under forty. Most people didn't worry about their financial security through a long old age. But as science dramatically expanded the number of years a man could expect to spend on this earth, the American Dream expanded too. Today, a long and satisfying retirement is as important in many people's minds as a successful career.

Like most Americans, I support a role for the government in providing a social safety net for Americans in great need, particularly seniors. The question since the days of Franklin Roosevelt and his New Deal has been how to construct it. Some believe that the government should be completely in charge, as it is under the current Social Security system. Others believe in a hybrid approach like the Medicare prescription drug program, which is publicly funded and governed, with the private sector delivering the benefits. Others favor government incentives, primarily through the tax code, for a privately operated system. And a few hardy libertarians prefer no government role at all.

What would the Founders think? Article I, Section 8, of the Constitution gives Congress the power to "provide for the common defense and general welfare" of the country. So clearly they envisioned some role for the federal government, but even the most enthusiastic Federalist would have imagined only a very limited one. I think a mixed approach, which employs both publicly funded and privately operated programs and incentivizes private charities, is the best and most comprehensive approach.

The two biggest federal programs are Social Security and Medicare.[5] Providing income support and healthcare for seniors and the disabled has become an accepted and assumed function of the federal government, even among conservatives. I'd ask anyone who seriously doubts this to name the last congressman or senator who ran on a platform of repealing either program.

Since Americans pay into the Social Security and Medicare systems throughout their working lives, they have a strong sense that they have *earned* the benefits that the system promises. The problem is that retirees are not drawing on the funds they socked away in a supposed "trust fund" while they worked. Their benefits are paid out of the current contributions of today's workers. A falling birthrate and increased longevity are leaving us with fewer workers to support the retirees. Under its current structure, the system won't be able to keep its promises for much longer. To make matters worse, Democrats treat the eighty-year-old existing system as sacrosanct, and they persecute deviation from orthodoxy with the zeal of a Torquemada.

Let's be clear, the greatest threat to Social Security and Medicare is the bankruptcy of the federal government. That will happen when we reach a point when the cost of the debt reaches a point where the government is no longer able to borrow without the market demanding structural spending reform. Look at Greece as an example. The first item on the chopping block when austerity is imposed will be entitlements, which account for more than 60 percent of the budget. The two biggest entitlements are Social Security and Medicare, with Medicaid (healthcare for low-income Americans, a majority of which is spent on seniors) a close third. Entitlements will put the government into insolvency, and they will be the target once that happens. No one wants that to happen, but only conservatives have been honest enough to level with the public. Unfortunately, we have no credibility with the public on these issues.

The fact is these programs are costly and inefficient in delivering help to the people most in need. Obamacare has been a spectacular reminder—if we needed one—that the government doesn't run a very efficient operation. When Uncle Sam is in charge, there is no accountability and little incentive to succeed. While Americans are gasping at the incompetence of a government-run healthcare system, we should push not only for the repeal of Obamacare but for the transformation of all the government healthcare programs, including Medicare and Medicaid. Americans expect a health insurance system that fosters medical innovation and expertise rather than destroying them. It must also provide for the medical needs of our vulnerable citizens. I'll discuss what we should do in chapter 7, but conservatives can take the lead on this momentous issue only if they affirm that the American Dream includes a secure retirement and that the federal government has a necessary, though not limitless, part to play.

———

The War on Poverty—supposedly one of the great achievements of postwar liberalism—has left behind a bloated, ineffective, and often destructive social welfare state. At the local level, cities like Washington and New York in the 1970s and 1980s, and more recently Detroit, Philadelphia, and Cleveland, have suffered terrible financial and social problems after years of applying this ideology under Democratic rule. Yet some Republicans think that poverty and the struggles of blue collar America are not a "winning" issue for our party. They should look at what the British Conservative Party has done in recent years. On the issue of poverty, the *Tories*, of all people, put the Labor Party on the defensive. We can do that here.

In the mid-2000s, Iain Duncan Smith, a Conservative member of Parliament, established a think tank called the Centre for Social Justice to study social breakdown in Great Britain and the poverty that followed.[6] After traveling around to many troubled communities, he wrote that he saw "levels of social breakdown which appalled me. In the fourth largest economy in the world, too many people lived in dysfunctional homes, trapped on benefits. Too many children were leaving school with no qualifications or skills to enable them to work and prosper. Too many communities were blighted by alcohol and drug addiction, debt and criminality, many of them with stunningly low levels of life expectancy."[7] Sound familiar? Mr. Duncan Smith was struck by how many people in those broken-down towns felt that politicians had given up on them and the political process had become irrelevant. Again, a familiar ring for Americans.

The goals of the Centre for Social Justice are remarkably similar to those affirmed in the American Declaration of Independence—that "each person, family and community is given every possible opportunity to reach their full potential." And they sought to achieve those goals by combining government policy making with the efforts of local volunteer organizations that are in the best position to provide direct and effective support.

The project identified five "pathways to poverty"—family breakdown (illegitimacy and divorce), educational failure, unemployment, addiction, and indebtedness. All the same root causes are at work here. The center's report, *Breakdown Britain*, formed the basis of Prime Minister David Cameron's social policy (Duncan Smith became the works and pensions secretary in Cameron's government) and produced new policies and mindsets. The report was followed by a set of proposals, *Breakthrough Britain*. The work of Duncan Smith is a great model for conservatives here in the United States.

———

While well-intentioned but corrosive welfare programs have taken their toll, the government is not entirely to blame for the deterioration of the American Dream. The mass entertainment industry—movies, television and radio, music, books and magazines, and now the internet, everything we commonly call "popular culture"—promotes with chilling effectiveness behavior, beliefs, and attitudes that are virtually guaranteed to produce unhappiness in individuals and families. That is why I took the position as CEO of EchoLight Studios, a faith and family movie production and distribution company. We need to fight back by producing and promoting high-quality films that present the good, the true, and the beautiful. And if we are going to give the average American a chance to succeed, we must win.

We all have learned in our history classes the influence of popular culture. In the 1700s, Thomas Paine's pamphlet *Common Sense* pushed Americans toward revolution. *Uncle Tom's Cabin* so stirred the conscience of the nation that it endured a civil war in order to extirpate slavery. From our earliest days, books and plays have helped define America. In words attributed to the seventeenth-century Scottish politician Andrew Fletcher, "If a man were permitted to make all the ballads, he need not care who should make the laws of a nation."[8]

The cultural toxins are brewed not only in Hollywood but also on Madison Avenue, which is perverting the American Dream of a prosperous life into a materialist nightmare. The pitchmen inflame our appetites with a degraded vision of the good life, usually sold with sex.

This American nightmare is a prescription for disillusionment, emptiness, and despair. The advertisers show you what you must have or must look like to be happy or beautiful. It's a lie, and the lie leads to bankruptcy and anorexia. Show me a single and sexually inactive man or woman in a movie, and I show you an unhappy, ridiculed loser. Show me the opposite extreme in real life, and I'll show you a lonely, vacuous predator or a willing victim who will likely struggle with meaningful romantic relationships, even within his or her marriage.

This egocentric pursuit of pleasure, material wealth, sex without consequences, and fame is the new morality. It may provide temporary thrills and moments of satisfaction, but it will not lead to happiness. The little band of patriots who pledged their lives, their fortunes, and their sacred honor in Philadelphia had something very different in mind when they declared that all men have a God-given right to the pursuit of happiness. They weren't talking about the pleasure of a contented animal. Noah Webster's first dictionary, published in 1828, defined happiness as "The agreeable sensations which spring from the enjoyment of good."[9] "Good," in turn, was defined as "having moral qualities best adapted to its design and use, or the qualities which God's law requires; virtuous; pious; religious."[10] Happiness means living in conformity with God's intention for your life. We are endowed by our Creator with the other two "unalienable rights" of life and liberty so that we may pursue his will for our life—to be good.

The root of the confused new morality is a grossly distorted understanding of freedom. We Americans like to talk about freedom, but we rarely examine what we mean by the word. In recent decades, it has become popular, particularly among many libertarians, to think of freedom as being allowed to do as we please. But there are two aspects of freedom: freedom *from* (we've got that one down) and freedom *for*. In other words, the exercise of freedom must be oriented to choosing what is true and good, always keeping in mind our obligations to one another and the common good. Otherwise, freedom degenerates into license, which ignores others and pursues self-interest alone. So smoking marijuana, hiring prostitutes, aborting your child, ignoring the poor, and doing whatever else gives you momentary pleasure, as long as no one else gets hurt, are mistaken for freedom. This is how many young people—bamboozled by Madison Avenue, movies, and television—now define the American Dream. When freedom is thus distorted, the good itself is obscured. It is confused with choice, and choice, irrespective of what is chosen, reigns supreme.

The cultural elites tell these lies about freedom to the rest of us, and the people who suffer the most from these lies are the ones who can't buy their way out of the neighborhoods that are ravaged by the resulting dysfunction. The music producers, Hollywood moguls, advertising executives, and politicians who subscribe to these lies will not be there to bail them out of jail, pay for rehab, help their children stay in school, or give them a job when their lives fall apart. They are too busy exercising their narrow, destructive view of freedom.

======

Achieving our dreams and building a better life for our family require tremendous work and commitment, but that is what makes them so worthwhile. The result most likely is good health, freedom from want, a strong and thriving family, and spiritual well-being. Not bad. We are the stewards of this. It's up to us to maintain this ideal and reject the unhealthy distortions our culture too often forces upon us.

The Harrisons know this. They never had illusions about wealth and fame, and they've taught their boys that success in life is not defined by how much disposable wealth you have and how famous you are. Those things are mirages, and they're dangerous for the people who pursue them. What the Harrisons want for their children are good jobs that allow them to live comfortably, strong families, and healthy values that include faith and giving back to the community. That's their American Dream.

======

Thinking about the problems we face—the economic and cultural threats to the American Dream—it's easy to become gloomy. Especially if, like the Harrisons and like me, you've got children who are going to inherit a nation whose promise seems dimmer than the one we inherited. That's a temptation we've got to resist. I like to recall the three greatest leaders on the world stage when I started my family and my career—Ronald Reagan, Margaret Thatcher, and John Paul II—the president, prime minister, and pope who, against all expectations, brought down the evil empire of Soviet communism. No one saw the world's problems more clearly or appreciated their gravity more thoroughly than those three extraordinary people. Their personalities and temperaments were very different, but none of them ever gave in to discouragement. It was not a matter of mere optimism, of a naturally sunny disposition, but of a deep faith in divine Providence. With the same faith, we will be equal to the challenges of our own time.

———

There are solutions to America's problems. We will have to work both from the bottom up and from the top down. Above all, we must be daring. Let's turn now to what we can do.

Marriage, family, community: This is where it all starts. Family is the basis. As Iain Duncan Smith showed, the number one "path to poverty" is family breakup. What are the core causes of this, and how do we address them? Family breakup is the result of poverty and a cause of poverty—it's a vicious circle with many victims. You won't hear a word about it from President Obama or the Democrats, or from many Republican for that matter. This is up to us as Americans to take care of.

Healthcare: President Obama's massive healthcare plan—Obamacare—is perhaps the biggest domestic threat confronting the American Dream today. This disastrous legislation is going to destroy the greatest healthcare system in the world and make Americans more, not less, dependent on our federal government. It fundamentally restructures the relationship between our government and our citizens for the worse.

Education: From early childhood education up through college and graduate education, we need to ensure that Americans have access to quality, affordable, and practical education. Our schools, riddled with apathy and clogged with bureaucracy, have fallen behind others in the world. It's unacceptable, and before we can have jobs and industry, we need education.

Industry and energy: It's simple. We need to create more opportunities for American workers. A generation ago a hardworking college or trade school graduate would find opportunities to earn good wages in exchange for hard work. This usually meant making things—manufacturing. Our automobile, steel, and textile industries were the biggest, but they have suffered from global economic forces and bad leadership. It is not about reviving these industries and bringing these jobs back; it's about getting the lion's share of the manufacturing of tomorrow's products. All of this will be fueled by what could be the biggest energy boom this country or any country has ever seen if President Obama isn't allowed to destroy it.

Taxing and spending: To preserve our safety net and create better jobs, our leaders need to reform the entitlement programs that are driving us into bankruptcy and reform the tax code to encourage hard work. We have to stop kidding ourselves about the weaknesses in the social safety net and stop kicking the can down the road for our kids to deal with. And we have to deal with a dysfunctional tax code that stymies growth and costs billions in compliance and enforcement.

Message: Words matter. Leadership matters. We need our leaders to stand up and inspire us. They need to believe our best days are yet to come before we can believe that. It's really important, and we are failing at it.

So let's begin. Where do we go from here?

CHAPTER SIX

GOVERNMENT CANNOT READ YOU A BEDTIME STORY

B ack in 1964, a time when the American Dream was much more vivid for middle- and low-income Americans, only 7 percent of children were born to unwed mothers.[1] Today that figure is almost 40 percent.[2] And while the poverty rate today for married families is 5 percent, for single-mother families it's over 40 percent.[3] Blue collar conservatives struggle to raise their kids with the right values, but because of economic and social circumstances, they are among the most at risk.

Let's go back to the Harrison family. James's older brother, Jeff, worked with him at the local aluminum plant. When Jeff was laid off, he briefly worked for an auto parts store—until the national chain closed it. He struggled to find a job that could support his family. Financial problems led to drinking problems and then marital problems. Jeff and his wife, Jackie, divorced. At the time, they had two preteen daughters.

With their parents separated and their mom working extra shifts at a call center thirty minutes away, the girls were left unsupervised for long periods and fell into a bad crowd from their high school. They began experimenting with alcohol and drugs. The older of the two daughters, Kathy, began failing in school and missing class frequently. The school barely noticed and never bothered to alert either parent. Jeff and Jackie had always tried to keep their kids away from drugs, alcohol, and sex, but they were drowned out by the internet, movies, TV, music, and peers, which all had a very different message. Last year, Kathy got pregnant. Now she's eighteen years old and has a baby but not a high school degree. The father of her child is also without a degree and has offered little financial or other help, acting as though it is not his responsibility.

What are Kathy's prospects, and what are her child's? There's no one else to take care of her baby, so Kathy won't be able to hold a job until her child is a few years older. Her mother and her father love her and want to support her but don't have much money. She recently went on food stamps and a program to help her with formula and diapers for the baby. Kathy fell into the safety net, and there she lies. How long will it take her to climb out of it? What will motivate her to do so?

———

If Kathy had grown up in a wealthy town like Charles Murray's Belmont, her father would never have lost his job—or he would have quickly found a new one. Her parents' marriage would probably still be intact. They would have been able to keep her focused on her schoolwork and other healthy activities. She would have been playing field hockey, studying Spanish, and doing volunteer work, all with an eye to college. Could she have gotten into trouble? Of course. Some kids in Belmont do, but unlike the parents in Fishtown, Belmont moms and dads have the resources to help pick up the pieces. That doesn't mean that kids in Belmont don't ever fail, but they have a much more extensive network of support to help them through the tough times.

The situation is most dire in African American communities. In 1965, Daniel Patrick Moynihan, then a young assistant secretary of labor, was one of the first to recognize the seriousness of this problem. In what became known as the "Moynihan Report," he argued that there was a strong link between the rise in single-parent families in the African American community and poverty.[4] At the time, the out-of-wedlock birthrate among blacks was 24 percent, and his argument was controversial. Today the rate is 73 percent, with 67 percent living without a father in the home. The correlation between illegitimacy, fatherlessness, and poverty is indisputable. Another worrying sign is that the illegitimacy rate among Hispanics has risen dramatically in recent years to over 50 percent.[5]

What is going on in these minority communities? The civil rights establishment and most liberals refuse to address this calamity. They blame racism. But no one can seriously argue that racism is more prevalent now than it was in the 1960s, and the correlation between poverty and high illegitimacy rates in black and Hispanic communities is as strong as any correlation you can find in social science. Breaking ranks with liberal orthodoxy, some prominent blacks today are willing to address the issue head-on. The film director Spike Lee recently had this to say in an interview with the *Washington Post*:

> Three out of four African American families are headed by a single mom. That's 75 percent. And I will put my left hand on 10 Bibles and my right hand to God and say that's the main correlation to the highest drop-out rate and the highest prison rate, and it manifests itself ultimately with these young brothers killing each other with this insane pathological genocide that's happening.... It all comes back to the fact that—and I'm not trying to demonize these single moms, they're doing the best

they can, working two or three jobs to keep it together. But these young boys, and young women, with no father in their lives, how can that not affect their relationship with black men? It's the domino effect.[6]

President Obama has occasionally struck the right tone too, telling a graduating class at Morehouse College, "Sure, go get your MBA, or start that business, we need black businesses out there. But ask yourself what broader purpose your business might serve, in putting people to work, or transforming a neighborhood.... Everything else is unfulfilled if we fail at family."[7]

We need more from him on this subject. Promoting responsible fatherhood, particularly in the black community, could be his greatest legacy, if he cared enough to do it. There is also an opportunity for the president to call on his friends in Hollywood to promote this message at least as strongly as they promote other topics, like global warming and same-sex unions. What's stopping them?

Talking about single motherhood and its effect on poverty is controversial because it hits so many people we know. Sometimes this is not a convenient argument for Republicans to make. Many of our leaders have been divorced too, including President Reagan. But the truth, as Al Gore might say, is not always convenient.

Children born into families with absent fathers are five times more likely to be poor. However heroic a particular single mother might be, children in homes without a father are up against heavy odds. They are more likely to be abused in the home, do poorly in school and drop out, commit a crime, use drugs and alcohol, have children out of wedlock, have lower incomes, and have more mental health problems than children raised with two parents. When I say they're more likely to have these problems, I mean *much* more likely.

The party that supposedly cares about the poor and downtrodden seems content with the palliative of a government check while it concentrates on the fashionable causes that engage high-income urban professionals. Never mind that many of these causes—abortion; the deconstruction of marriage; and the extirpation of religion from schools, the culture, and public life, for example—have already had a devastating effect on lower-income America.[8]

Single mothers aren't the only ones to suffer from these developments. They have been a catastrophe for men as well. Research from organizations like the Third Way, a liberal think tank, shows that men, especially poorly educated men, have fallen behind women in many important areas. For example, college attendance for men has declined while it has increased for women, and women have surpassed men in earning both college and post-graduate degrees. The loss of low-skill, blue collar jobs once held mostly by men has driven down real wages for men while wages have grown for women. A Third Way study titled *Wayward Sons* finds a strong correlation between a boy's growing up in a single family and the chances of his finishing high school and going to college. Broken families hurt boys more than girls, making them less likely to become good earners and strong husbands and fathers—the vicious cycle again.[9]

There's another cause of broken families over which we have some control. Astonishingly, 2.7 million American children have a parent in prison, the vast majority of them fathers. The prison population has exploded in recent years because of mandatory sentencing guidelines and three-strike laws. We are putting too many people in jail, and it's doing enormous damage at a time when we desperately need stronger families. Conservatives on the state level have been leading the way on reforming sentencing laws for certain nonviolent offenders with an eye to the larger picture.[10]

If we don't restore the family, the foundation of society, the superstructure will collapse. We have already seen this happen in communities where there are no marriages and no dads. One obvious cure to this illness is the healing medicine that comes from churches and other volunteer and charitable organizations. One of my favorite ministries helps families dealing with the trauma of an unexpected and unwanted pregnancy. Pregnancy care clinics around the country serve not just women in crisis, but their families, and increasingly the fathers of their unborn children.

On an early campaign swing through Spartanburg, South Carolina, I met a force of nature, Alexia Newman, who, twenty-four years ago, became director of Carolina Pregnancy Center. At that time, it was a tiny place that had gone through five directors in three years. The year before her arrival, the center had worked with 139 clients on an annual budget of just $36,000. Alexia immediately expanded the hours of the clinic and was able to help more than six times as many people in her first year as director.

Today, the eight-thousand-square-foot facility is still run on a shoestring budget, but it now serves more than 2,600 people a year. I can only imagine how many lives have been saved and families healed because of Alexia and her team's commitment. The center provides pregnancy tests, ultrasounds, advice for pregnant women, counseling for those who have had abortions or miscarriages, a mentoring program, parenting classes for moms and dads, fatherhood classes, and even a loan closet for maternity and baby clothing. Want to know how you can help build a culture of life and help young, struggling families? Look to Alexia. It doesn't take the millions of dollars in government funding that Planned Parenthood gets. It just takes love, commitment, and a desire to help.

———

There is no denying that we face strong cultural headwinds. Our marriage rate is at a record low.[11] Marriage is seen as a temporary lifestyle choice, not the foundation of society.

Many people are deferring it, and many others are dropping it entirely. That's not good news for our children or our future. In fact, we have seen that if the family retreats, the government will take its place. Parents have authority over their children because they are responsible for them. As the government takes over that responsibility for some children, it will try to assume that authority for all children. A comment by MSN-BC's Melissa Harris-Perry reveals where we're headed: "We have to break through our kind of private idea that kids belong to their parents or kids belong to their families, and recognize that kids belong to whole communities."[12]

Despite the mountain of evidence that strong families are the best antipoverty program, many liberals, blinded by ideology, peddle the fantasy that children will be fine in almost any conceivable domestic arrangement. A famous controversy two decades ago showed us how ferociously they will defend that delusion. When the protagonist of the popular TV show *Murphy Brown*, a liberal news anchorwoman, deliberately chose to have a child out of wedlock, Vice President Dan Quayle, in a speech delivered shortly after the 1992 Los Angeles riots, criticized the message the show was sending. Addressing the breakdown of many black families, Quayle said, "Bearing babies irresponsibly is simply wrong. Failing to support children one has fathered is wrong, and we must be unequivocal about this. It doesn't help matters when prime-time TV has Murphy Brown, a character who supposedly epitomizes today's intelligent, highly paid, professional woman, mocking the importance of fathers by bearing a child alone and calling it just another lifestyle choice. I know it is not fashionable to talk about moral values, but … it's time to make the discussion public."[13]

Quayle's remarks did not go over well. He was ridiculed by the late-night talk-show hosts and political pundits as out of touch, sexist, and racist. "How dare he suggest such a thing?" was the common refrain from Hollywood, feminists, and Democrats in Congress. Eventually, in 1993, a brave social scientist named Barbara Dafoe Whitehead changed the tone of the controversy with an article in the *Atlantic* titled "Dan Quayle Was Right." There was actually strong evidence from social science to support Quayle's views, she wrote, and now, more than twenty years later, the evidence is overwhelming and unmistakable.[14] But have you heard many—or any—liberal apologies to Dan Quayle? More important, have you heard any liberal apologies for all the lives they've wrecked through their policies and the messages they've sent through our popular culture?

Now, I recognize that rebuilding our families isn't something our government can legislate very well, but for starters we can at least remove the perverse incentives in many government programs that discourage marriage. Our public schools used to take it for granted that they were educating future mothers and fathers who needed to be prepared to take on the future responsibilities of parenthood. That meant developing a work ethic, learning personal responsibility, and acquiring the skills necessary to hold down a job.

Our political leaders should express their support for marriage and family. President Obama demonstrated the power of his "bully pulpit" when his endorsement of same-sex marriage contributed to the dramatic change in public opinion on the issue. What if he used his considerable influence in favor of a child's right to be raised by both parents in a home founded on the commitment of marriage?

———

When I was a congressman, I was one of the principal authors of the welfare reform proposal in the Republicans' 1994 Contract with America. I was elected to the Senate that year, and I decided to practice what I preached by hiring five people for my staff who were on welfare, food stamps, or other government aid. One was Billy Jo, a girl not long out of high school and already a mother of two children. She was attending a community college part-time and receiving subsidized childcare at a first-rate facility in Harrisburg. I hired her to work part-time in my Harrisburg office while she finished her degree. We didn't realize then that after a year of working in my office she would lose her subsidized childcare benefit.

She was an outstanding employee, but she resigned when faced with the loss of her benefits; she simply could not get by without childcare. She had no extended family to call on for support, for she was also the child of a single mother.

That is another unspoken advantage of stable two-parent homes—there are a lot more grandparents, aunts, uncles, and cousins who are connected to you. That is a social safety net of its own—extended families look after and support each other. But in Billy Jo's case, the family was fractured, and her older, unemployed sister was, initially, not inclined to help. But just as we were about to say our sad farewells, Billy Jo's sister had a change of heart and decided she could watch the children, because she wanted to help the sister she loved. By her act of service, she not only helped Billy Jo but she got her own life back on track. In a family and in a community, charity benefits the giver as well as the recipient. That doesn't happen in a government program. Billy Jo finished her degree and became a schoolteacher. But what would have happened to her, to her sister, and to the kids' relationship with their extended family if the government had stepped in? Everyone would have been made poorer where it really matters. Family makes us stronger.

—————

In too many neighborhoods, single motherhood has become a norm passed down from generation to generation. If we want to change that, we can start by reemphasizing the importance of two-parent families. Imagine if instead of expending enormous amounts of time and money trying to redefine marriage, we had channeled all that passion into a national discussion about the importance to all of society for men and women to get married before having children? What if government agencies produced ads showing the truth—that married people are happier or more successful or any number of positive attributes for individuals and society? Imagine the news media, Hollywood, businesses, schools, and political activists joining with government at all levels to form a national consensus about having children after marriage and the importance of building healthy marriages. There might be no bigger step toward restoring the American Dream.

This has been done on a small scale in several communities around the country. When I was in the Senate, I asked a group to testify before my committee about their efforts in Chattanooga, Tennessee, to encourage marriage before having children, reduce illegitimacy, help hold together existing marriages, and promote the importance of healthy marriages. First Things First worked with schools, churches, government, businesses, and the media. This effort has resulted in a 62 percent decrease in unwed teen pregnancies and a 29 percent reduction in divorce.

Churches and organizations like First Things First hold the key to a marriage revolution in lower-income communities. The top income earners in the country have figured out the importance of marriage. According to Charles Murray, roughly 80 percent of wealthy thirty- to fifty-year-olds are married, a figure that has declined only slightly in forty years. Among their low-income counterparts, the marriage rate is about half that. Don't you think it is time for the elites in our society, including the elites in government, to preach what they practice?

But there is one more thing government can do, or better yet, one *less* thing—quit trying to replace the family with cradle-to-grave government programs. Some will object that I've got cause and effect mixed up. Did more government assistance cause the breakdown of the family, or did the breakdown of the family require more government assistance? Let's review the numbers. Look at the out-of-wedlock birth rate in 1964, the year the War on Poverty was launched with the passage of a permanent food stamp program, which was followed by Medicare, Medicaid, and an expansion of other welfare benefits in the late '60s and early 1970s.

From 1930 to 1960, the rate of out-of-wedlock births was remarkably constant—around 3 to 5 percent. From 1960 to 1965, it started to rise gradually, reaching 7 percent in 1965. In the next twenty years, it went to 22 percent and jumped to 33 percent in 1995. The rate flattened out over the next ten years and then began its ascent again from 2005 to the current rate of over 40 percent. So in only one period during the last forty years did the increase in the rate of out-of-wedlock births abate, the ten-year period after the passage of the Welfare

Reform Act of 1996. That act required work and put a time limit on the receipt of income assistance for unwed mothers. It also required the establishment of paternity in order for the father to take better responsibility for his children. By 2006 many of these reforms had been watered down by big liberal states like New York and California. President Obama, with his mighty authoritarian pen, has made it worse.

Obviously, there are other more important factors affecting the illegitimacy rate—the sexual revolution, birth control, abortion, the popular culture, and much more. Government policy, however, is at least facilitating the dramatic decline in stable two-parent families through what on the surface seems to be compassionate assistance for families in crisis. That is why reforming these programs by adding work requirements, putting a limit on benefits, and reintegrating the father into the picture, if possible, is essential to stop this slide.

The great British statesman Edmund Burke—America's greatest friend in Parliament as the colonies' grievances against the mother country grew in the years before the Revolution—insisted on the importance of society's "little platoons"—the myriad associations and communities through which men conduct most of the important business of life. They constitute the bonds of a healthy society, and because they are the essential buffer between individual citizens and the state, they are the guarantors of freedom. The primary little platoon is the family. For America to be strong and free, we must have strong families.

And strong families often rely on churches. The correlation between regular church attendance and strong marriages and healthy families is thoroughly established. Regular church attendance also correlates with far lower levels of crime, addiction, and depression.

Dr. Patrick Fagan of the Family Research Council has collated all the data and can show that married couples who do not attend church are twice as likely to divorce as married couples who attend church regularly. Moreover, churchgoing kids are far more likely to do well in school (especially poor children) and to be better behaved. And churchgoing families are far more likely to be involved in community and volunteer work. Dr. Fagan concludes, "No other dimension of life in America—with the exception of stable marriages and families, which in turn are strongly tied to religious practice—does more to promote the well-being and soundness of the nation's civil society than citizens' religious observance.... Social science data reinforce George Washington's declaration in his farewell address: 'Of all the dispositions and habits which lead to political prosperity, Religion and Morality are indispensable supports.'"[15] Instead of President Obama's war against faith-filled businesses, not-for-profits, and individuals, why don't we do something really radical and talk about religion's civic and personal benefits?

If George Washington could say it, why can't we? Why can't our policy makers come to grips with the simple fact, illustrated in social science data and throughout our history, that strong families and strong churches make a strong nation? Reality, after all, is the most reliable guide for policy.

CHAPTER SEVEN

REPLACE OBAMACARE BEFORE IT'S TOO LATE

The government should provide a safety net for the aged, infirm, and disabled. As we know, almost half of our population now receives some sort of government benefit. That wasn't good enough for President Obama and his power-hungry cronies. They simply do not trust free markets and capitalism to create wealth efficiently and effectively and to allocate it fairly. So the progressives have been on a march for a century to replace capitalism with a command-and-control economic model according to which the government designs and heavily regulates the marketplace.

They have enjoyed conspicuous success in the field of healthcare. Prior to President Obama's taking office in 2009, nearly half of the payments for medical care in this country were already made by either federal, state, or local government.[1] The dominant player in the market, government, had a huge effect on cost, quality, and access to care. In spite of this heavy hand, the private side of the healthcare system still managed to be innovative in delivering healthcare more efficiently and effectively, though it was hobbled compared with other industries. Then Barack Obama burst onto the scene and forced through the ironically named "Patient Protection and Affordable Care Act," a law that most Americans now realize is threatening patients and making care less affordable. This law brings private health insurance directly under the command of the federal government. In a 2,500-plus-page bill, followed by thousands upon thousands of pages of regulations, the government now is going to design all insurance policies and the market in which they are sold. It is going to impose mandates on employers to provide coverage and penalties on individuals and businesses if they don't buy government-approved coverage. Government-appointed oversight boards will attempt to keep a lid on prices and limit the overhead costs of insurance companies. And that's just the beginning.

Obamacare will reshape the relationship between government and the people to resemble that in Western Europe, where the vast majority depend on the government for their healthcare. Like any dependency, it is painful and indeed almost impossible to break. The promise of healthcare for all provided by the largesse of the federal government will not make us stronger. It will lead to less innovation and fewer cures. For all but the wealthiest, it will result in less choice of caregivers, longer lines, higher costs, and lower-quality medicine than a private system.

Worst of all, it will give the government more power than it has ever had over all but the wealthiest Americans. Government will control who lives and who dies, who gets care, how much he gets, and when he gets it. We are about to hand to our children a country less free than we found it, and for what?

When President Obama was elected, there were approximately forty-five million uninsured persons in this country, yet everyone in America was guaranteed the best medical care in the world at any hospital in the country.[2] If you believe the optimistic projections by the Congressional Budget Office, which so far has underestimated costs and overestimated the number of people insured under Obamacare, in ten years the government will spend an additional $1.36 trillion on healthcare, but there will still be thirty million uninsured, and many people will be receiving inferior coverage and care.[3]

As we all know, the Obamacare rollout was an embarrassing disaster. People trying to buy plans on the new government exchanges spent frustrating hours at the computer—in some cases, they had to keep coming back for days and even weeks—and many gave up altogether. Weeks after the launch, it was revealed that 40 percent of the system, including the crucial part needed to process payments to insurance companies, hadn't even been built.[4] But it gets worse. As January 2014 arrived, hundreds of thousands of Americans who thought they had enrolled arrived at a doctor's office only to learn that even after all they had endured, they had no coverage. Perhaps worst of all, more and more Americans who have successfully enrolled are discovering that many of our country's best doctors and hospitals simply do not participate in these Obamacare health plans.[5]

Despite President Obama's now infamous promise, millions of Americans are losing the insurance plans they liked.[6] According to the Obama administration's own 2010 estimate (back when the president was still disingenuously promising that you could keep your current insurance), upward of 5.6 million Americans who bought their policies on the individual market would have them canceled because of Obamacare regulations. And sure enough, in 2013, millions of people received letters telling them their plans were canceled because they weren't in compliance with Obamacare's new standards.

Even the *Washington Post*'s "Fact Checker," which bends over backward to defend Obamacare, concedes that 4.7 million Americans had their plans canceled.[7] Another wave of cancellations, hitting people who work for small businesses, is on deck.

On January 24, 2014, the administration announced that three million people had signed up for plans on the Obamacare exchanges. Only a tiny percentage of the total signups, however—possibly as little as 10 percent—were people who had been uninsured before Obamacare. So on top of breaking an insurance system that was working for millions of Americans, Obamacare has done pathetically little to solve the problems of the uninsured. According to Gallup, a bigger percentage of Americans say they're uninsured now than when President Obama was elected in 2008.[8]

To understand the true damage inflicted by Obamacare, though, you have to hear some of the stories of the millions it has affected. The story of Ken and Melissa Davert of Bangor Township, Michigan, was reported by their local television news.[9] They are married with fifteen-year-old twins, Austin and Michaela. All four family members have serious medical problems. Ken has cerebral palsy, and his wife and children suffer from osteogenesis imperfecta, which causes severe bone and lung problems.

The Davert parents had been covered by Medicare, and they had a private insurance policy they liked for their children. Despite the president's promise, they lost their Blue Cross policy to Obamacare. They tried to buy a new policy on the exchange, but their application was first lost and then denied. And then they were left for months to hear the result of their appeal of the denial. Meanwhile, they need coverage for their twins. So they have bought a new Blue Cross policy that complies with Obamacare—quadrupling their exposure to out-of-pocket costs to a frightening $10,200 per person.

The Daverts asked their senators and congressman for help. An employee of the Department of Health and Human Services who heard their story called to let them know that their problems might be due to a computer "glitch" causing "applicants who potentially may be eligible for Medicaid to be denied coverage." *A computer glitch.*

The Daverts thought they were not eligible for Medicaid because they had jobs. But Obamacare is going to push lots of people who used to be able to pay for private insurance onto Medicaid. According to Jim Capretta of the Ethics and Public Policy Center, "The system will automatically sign them up for Medicaid, even if they don't want to be on Medicaid…. [A] lot of people are getting signed up for Medicaid just by virtue of what their income is."[10]

In November 2013, Nicole Hopkins reported in the *Wall Street Journal* that her mother, Charlene Hopkins, of Pierce County, Washington, had her insurance canceled. The Obamacare-compliant plan her insurer offered in its place was more expensive, because it included coverage the fifty-two-year-old woman didn't need: "maternity needs, newborn wellness and pediatric dental care." So she tried to buy a plan on the state's insurance exchange. The one and only option she was offered was enrollment in Medicaid. And "offered" is a polite way of putting what actually happened to her. While she thought she was still just exploring her options on the website, Charlene Hopkins was automatically signed up for Medicaid.

That was hard for Charlene to take: "'I just don't expect anything positive out of getting free health care,' she said. 'I don't see why other people should have to pay for my care.' In paying for health insurance herself—she won't accept help from her family, either—she was safeguarding her dignity and independence." As her daughter pointed out, Charlene Hopkins "has been forced to join the government-reliant poor, though she would prefer to contribute her two mites. The authorities behind 'affordable care' had erased her right to calculate what she was willing to spend to preserve her dignity—to determine what *she* thinks is affordable…. The Affordable Care Act is at risk of systematizing learned helplessness by telling individuals like my mother that they cannot afford to care for themselves in the way they could before the law was enacted. 'This makes me feel poorer than ever,' she said."[11]

Our federal government should not be forcing independent citizens like Charlene Hopkins into welfare programs. It should not be yanking affordable, dependable private insurance out from under struggling families with serious medical problems like the Daverts. Americans want a hand up, not a handout. But instead of lifting people up, Obamacare is pushing countless Americans down into a state of dependency, uncertainty, and reliance on the whims of bureaucrats.

There's no shame in relying on the government's safety net in cases of true need. But it is an outrage for government artificially to create that "need" by forcing the cancellation of private insurance policies.

Obamacare is more than the ultimate expression of the Washington-knows-best mentality; it includes a direct assault on the freedom of religion guaranteed in the First Amendment. The president has gone so far as to tell the Little Sisters of the Poor that they have to buy coverage for contraception and abortion in violation of their consciences.

———

Having asserted control over practically every aspect of healthcare in America, the Obama administration should be held responsible for the shameful results we've already seen—and for the worse that is to come. But the president continues to make excuses for the Obamacare debacle. He blames Republicans, suggesting that we have proposed no alternative, that we're denying the very real problems that afflicted the healthcare system *before* Obamacare. That's simply not accurate.

In 1992, when I was a freshman congressman, John Kasich and I introduced the first health savings account bill. HSAs put consumers in charge of their routine care and gave them the incentive to be wise purchasers of services. If you spend your money and time to stay healthy, *you* receive the financial benefit, not the insurance company. Although the idea has never been fully implemented in Washington, in states that have passed it, costs have gone down, and satisfaction up. When this patient-centered approach has been tried with Medicaid recipients, whom the Left believes are incapable of making wise healthcare choices, the results have been encouraging.

One of the key problems with Obamacare is that it doubles down on the idea that Washington can impose a one-size-fits-all solution in healthcare. The reality is that states have developed the most effective healthcare policies. The demographics of the uninsured and the conditions affecting healthcare costs and access are simply different in South Carolina than in New York or Colorado or Alaska. And because of their different political climates and cultures, the citizens of those states are likely to respond to different incentives and develop different approaches. This fundamental truth is why I support changing the current Medicaid program to more of a block-grant system that would provide states much more flexibility than they have today to design innovative programs to address the problems of the uninsured.

We can also help our fellow citizens burdened with preexisting conditions without disrupting the insurance market for the vast majority of those who are happy with their current plan. "High-risk pools" are programs that provide a mechanism for extending coverage to those facing these chronic health conditions. The traditional problem with state high-risk pools, however, is that the premiums are unaffordable.

Furthermore, these pools usually provide only an insurance card, with no education or guidance to patients on how best to take care of themselves to achieve better health and a longer, more fruitful life. Another way to help the uninsurable is to provide states the opportunity to access federal funds in addition to their Medicaid block grant to create state-based programs. For a state's program to qualify, it would have to meet a limited set of criteria designed to maximize state flexibility, while addressing the problems of high premiums and education and ensuring accountability to patients and taxpayers:

1. Provide at least one avenue for those with preexisting conditions to obtain insurance coverage at no more than 125 percent of the average price for individual health insurance in the state;

2. Include in the coverage plan for this population a meaningful education and care management component; and

3. Create a continuous-improvement program to monitor results and cost, ensuring that patients are getting the healthcare they need and taxpayers are investing in something that works.

Once we have addressed those with preexisting conditions, we must unleash the power of competition and free markets to create more choices and lower costs for traditional insurance consumers. Enhanced competition in both the number of carriers in the market and in the types of products available will drive innovation and help control costs.

In exchange for the federal funds in the block-grant program, I would ask states to take two other important steps to provide citizens and small businesses a greater number of choices:

1. Allow carriers to offer at least one policy that is free from expensive coverage mandates. This will allow people, not the government, to balance coverage and cost, and to shop for products that meet their individual needs at prices they can afford; and

2. Adopt a uniform licensing process for out-of-state insurance companies to make it easier to sell insurance across state lines, while preserving the important consumer protection role of state government.

States are already taking the lead in creating innovative programs designed to improve the health of their citizens. In Iowa, where I have spent so much time, Governor Terry Branstad launched the "Healthiest State Initiative" in August 2011. He has a five-year goal of moving his state from nineteenth to first in the Gallup-Healthways Well-Being Index, which measures physical, mental, and emotional wellness. The program engages individuals, families, businesses, faith-based organizations, not-for-profits, and the public sector in a community-focused effort to educate citizens on healthy habits and to change behavior. The results are telling. By the 2012 report, Iowa had climbed ten spots to number nine, and I suspect they will climb even farther when the 2013 numbers are released.[12]

South Carolina had the fourth-highest percentage of premature babies in the nation in 2011, and one in every ten babies was admitted to a neonatal intensive care unit (NICU). Tony Keck, the state's director of health and human services, decided to tackle this problem head on. In July 2011, he created the "Birth Outcome Initiative" in collaboration with Blue Cross Blue Shield of South Carolina, the South Carolina Hospital Association, the March of Dimes, and others. The group developed several approaches, including payment reform, to improve the quality of care to moms and babies. By the first quarter of 2013, the program had already reduced NICU admissions and documented $6 million in savings for Medicaid.[13]

The federal government needs to encourage and support more of this state-level innovation rather than creating roadblocks to it and dictating one approach for everyone.

The federal tax code is an obstacle to sound healthcare reform, discriminating against citizens who buy their own medical insurance instead of getting it through an employer.

When I served in the Senate, I proposed a major reform that would have ended this discrimination by allowing individuals to buy insurance with pretax dollars just as companies do for their employees. I'm proud that this idea has become a key feature of the plan to replace Obamacare introduced by my old colleagues Senators Tom Coburn, Orrin Hatch, and Richard Burr. You'd think this would be a no-brainer—especially for the Democrats, who pride themselves on being the champions of the "little guy" against the corporations. How can they defend allowing corporations and other employers to buy insurance tax-free for their employees but not individuals?

This unequal tax treatment is at the root of the pre-Obamacare problems in our healthcare system that the president keeps referring to. Beginning in 1942, when President Franklin Roosevelt excluded insurance benefits from his wartime freeze on wages, and accelerating in 1954, when Congress made those benefits tax-free, the nature of health insurance has changed. To take advantage of the anomaly in the tax code, employers began giving employees prepaid routine medical care through "insurance" policies that were no longer actually insurance in the classic sense. As many pundits have pointed out, if we had the same kind of "insurance" for our cars as we now have for our health, the insurance company would pay for all our gas—and we'd have very little incentive to be careful of how much we spent on it!

Whenever a third party (an insurance company or the government) is paying, costs are bound to skyrocket. Why does laser vision-correction surgery keep getting cheaper while other kinds of medical care get ever more expensive? Well, vision-correcting eye surgery typically isn't covered by insurance. Patients pay for it themselves directly in the free market, and they demand better prices and service. In America today most people aren't even paying directly for their insurance, let alone most of their actual care.

A true revolution in healthcare would not increase the role of government, as Obamacare does, but make healthcare more like the industries that continue to give us more innovation at cheaper prices. There are certain things the government simply can't do as well as the private sector. The medical field requires a more dynamic solution that only private industry can provide.

Compare medicine with telecommunications, for example. Can you imagine if President Clinton had decided in the 1990s that everyone should have a cell phone? Since they were so expensive, he might have proposed that the government pay for everyone to have the phone that the Federal Communications Commission decided was best for him. Since the government would be guaranteeing everyone a cell phone and subsidizing it, the people who got BlackBerry devices and Motorolas would have to pay extra, and those companies would be taxed to support the program. In addition, the law

might give the government the power to tax expensive innovations that regulators thought unnecessary—like phones
with cameras, music, videos, internet, or apps. Absurd, right?

That's what Obamacare is doing to healthcare. Why, for
example, have we imposed a punishing new tax on medical
device manufacturers? These are the companies that make
replacement hips and knees and devices used in heart surgery—the procedures that have allowed American seniors to
live active lives rather than being confined to nursing homes
and wheelchairs. You get less of what you tax. Why would we
want less lifesaving medical innovation for the future? Whatever the problems of American healthcare before Obamacare,
Americans have benefited for decades from the innovation of
the medical device manufacturers. This is one American
industry that we can still be proud of—and Obama wants to
cripple it. The new tax is not even a tax on profits; it's on all
of a manufacturer's revenue, even if that manufacturer's business is running at a loss. In other words, a medical device
manufacturer can be a startup developing new products and
not yet making a penny of profit, and it still gets hit by the tax.
As former Congressional Budget Office director Douglas
Holtz-Eakin reports, this Obamacare tax is already hurting
companies and eliminating jobs. In Michigan, for example,
Stryker Instruments has laid off a thousand workers.[14] And
Cook Medical of Indiana is holding off on building five new
plants it had planned.[15]

And that's not the only way Obamacare is contributing to unemployment. It's also hurting the economy as a whole. Obamacare will "destroy the foundation of the 40 hour work week that is the backbone of the American middle class," according to a July 2013 letter from the presidents of the International Brotherhood of Teamsters and two other big unions. "Perverse incentives" in Obamacare that the union presidents pointed to include "an incentive for employers to keep employees' work hours below 30 hours a week. Numerous employers have begun to cut workers' hours to avoid this obligation, and many of them are doing so openly."[16] As Betsy McCaughey explains, the Labor Department actually reported "the shortest average work week on record" from January 1 to July 31 of 2013.[17] That was when large employers were anticipating that the mandate to buy insurance for any employee working more than thirty hours a week would go into effect on January 1, 2014, as Congress wrote in the law.

In fact, the employer mandate never went into effect, which brings us to another complaint in the union presidents' letter and something that should alarm anyone who cares about a constitutional government of laws not men. Obamacare gives the administration, particularly the secretary of health and human services, enormous powers. But this administration has not been satisfied with the powers that the law actually confers. The president has taken it upon himself unilaterally to "waive" and even alter various provisions of the law.

Under our Constitution, the president of the United States is not supposed to pick and choose which laws he's going to enforce. He may not amend, on his own motion, laws that Congress has duly passed. And yet repeatedly this president has simply decreed that he's not going to enforce certain parts of Obamacare. He has unilaterally moved deadlines and changed criteria that are expressly written in the bill that Congress passed and he signed into law.

In their letter, the union presidents complained that the administration had made a "huge accommodation for the employer community" in moving back the deadline for the employer mandate to go into effect while refusing to grant waivers of provisions that were hurting union members, provisions that might even destroy their healthcare plans. The Democrats pose as the friends of blue collar workers. They're supposed to be the unions' champions. Greedy Republicans, in contrast, are supposed to care only about big business and the rich. But the reality of Obamacare is that it's the Democrats who are stiffing workers.

Why are the Democrats catering to big corporations while making life more difficult for ordinary working people? The answer would seem to be that no matter how much they say they care about working Americans, the Democrats' real priority is putting more of everyone's lives under their control because they know what is best for everyone. When that priority comes into conflict with the needs of ordinary Americans, grabbing more power always wins.

In Obamacare we've taken a huge step toward a European-style system of socialized healthcare for America. And we can't afford it. How much fiscal sense does it make to force people like Charlene Hopkins, who was paying $276 a month for insurance she liked and could afford, onto Medicaid, where all her medical expenses will be billed to the taxpayers? In an even more absurd case, a retired Virginia man with a five-million-dollar home and three cars was told that Medicaid was his only Obamacare option. Forcing people who can afford to pay their own way into free government programs is the high road to national ruin. As Margaret Thatcher liked to say, the problem with socialism is that sooner or later you run out of other people's money.

But that isn't the only problem with big-government, top-down, centralized solutions, as Thatcher herself saw. She also argued that European-style socialism is immoral and corrupting. Obamacare is already turning independent citizens into the wards of the state—something our government has no right to do.

Nor does the government have the right to ration medicine, as it certainly will do once the expenses of this enormous new program begin to overrun the budget. Sarah Palin got a lot of flak for talking about "death panels," but Howard Dean, the former chairman of the Democratic National Committee, let the cat out of the bag, calling Obamacare's Independent Payment Advisory Board (IPAB) "essentially a health-care rationing body" for Medicare patients: "The IPAB will be able to stop certain treatments its members do not favor by simply setting rates to levels where no doctor or hospital will perform them."[18] As the father of a special-needs little girl, Bella, I know all too well who will be the target of healthcare rationing: those whose lives are not worth spending money on—the chronically ill, the very old, and the severely disabled. The Democrats in Congress were so anxious to free IPAB from having to answer to future Congresses—and thus, in future elections, to the American people—that they wrote into the Obamacare law a blatantly unconstitutional provision that the part of the law creating IPAB could be repealed only in January 2017.

Obamacare goes against who we are as a free people. In the fight to repeal it and replace it with genuine reform, Republicans are solidly on the side of working Americans, who want to be responsible for their own families and help their fellow citizens in true need—not become helpless victims of a government-knows-best system.

CHAPTER EIGHT

INNOVATING AND PERSONALIZING EDUCATION

James and Susan Harrison's son Jason is sixteen, and his brother, Thomas, is fourteen. Both have grown up going to the local public schools, playing Little League baseball, and participating in community service and camping trips with their church youth group. The boys could be described as fairly typical kids for this part of the country. They follow the Cleveland Indians, play their music too loud, and spend a lot of time playing Madden, NBA 2K, and other video games. Jason and Thomas are bright kids and have done reasonably well in school, but so far they have not gotten the high grades or test scores that would allow them to rely on scholarships to pay for college. Their parents think the boys haven't been pushed or challenged much by their teachers.

The performance of the local school has declined over the years, and the administration has turned over repeatedly, but the Harrisons have tried to stay involved. They've made sure Jason, who has an interest in computers and electronics, is a member of the computer club and enrolled in computer science courses, and they've tried to supplement his education by buying computer programming books. They regularly meet with Thomas's teachers to see if there is a way they can help improve his scores. The Harrisons don't feel they know the current principal very well, and it's hard to find time to talk to the teachers. But they try, and still they wonder if this is the best they can do for their boys.

Without the income they once had, they can't afford the local Catholic high school at $11,500 per year for each child. They would qualify for some aid, but even with that it's a stretch. The Harrisons worry about the quality of the education their kids are getting but also about some of the things they are exposed to in the school. It's not only the problems other kids bring from home, but the politically correct values that permeate the school. Let's put it this way, the boys aren't learning the history and citizenship lessons that James and Susan were taught when they were in school. Now they keep hearing about something called the Common Core standards, which seem to be pushed by the same people who made the public schools so mediocre in the first place. They can't help being suspicious.

With Jason in the middle of his junior year, the Harrisons' anxiety has grown over what will come next for him. Neither James nor Susan went on to college. But they know that the path to financial security for their kids now runs through some form of higher education. Fortunately, Jason is doing well enough academically to go to a four-year college, but paying for it is another matter. They read about the enormous costs of college and the heavy debt burdens many carry for years after finishing and wonder whether it is even the best choice. Would he be better off working and going to community college or even to a vocational program that would cost less and lead to more-immediate job opportunities?

The Harrisons know there is much less room for error than when they were growing up. Back then you followed a simple formula—stay in school, work reasonably hard, graduate, go to work. Today that's just a start.

Which raises an even deeper question: What is education all about? The Harrisons wonder if their kids are mastering the basic skills they need to get and hold a job—reading, writing, and math. But they also worry if they're developing the values that will make them good men. Making a good living is an extremely important goal and a darn good reason to go to school, but James and Susan know that simply having more stuff won't make their sons happy. Shouldn't the boys' education help them to be good citizens, good neighbors, good husbands and fathers, and simply *good men*? It's hard to see how four years on a typical American college campus will do that.

There are a few colleges, nevertheless, that do get it right, and I'm happy to say that one of them is Grove City College, in my home state of Pennsylvania. When I had the opportunity to deliver the commencement address there in 1998, I considered the purpose of higher education:[1]

A few years ago, a survey was taken of Japanese and American mothers. They were asked the question: "What do you want your children to be when they grow up?" The Japanese mothers said that they wanted their children to be successful. The overwhelming majority of American mothers said they didn't care what their children were as long as they were happy. I don't believe they really meant that they only wanted their children to be "happy"—at least I hope they didn't believe that. I can't imagine any of you mothers dropping off your child here as a freshman and, before leaving, looking them in the eye and saying: "Now go and be the happiest student at Grove City College." If any mothers did that, I am quite certain that they are not here today to witness their child's graduation! Do we really want the focus of children's lives, our lives, to be the pursuit of pleasure, of happiness? I grew up in an Italian-American household, and I can tell you my Italian father did not care if I was happy. What my mom and dad always said was: "Now Rick, you be good." I knew what good meant. It meant that there was a moral code that was based on universal truth. I'm afraid that, as a culture, we don't believe this anymore.

What has happened to the moms and dads who want their children to be good? I believe they are casualties of the cultural war in this country. We live now in a country that believes we should be non-judgmental to the point that we won't even fight for the souls of our own children. In my day, parents who fought for the souls of their children were called strict parents; now they are called right-wing radicals. Behavior that was once an affront to the basic moral code, a code grounded in truth, is now publicly accepted. Those who want to curb such behavior, or question such behavior, are dismissed as intolerant.

We live in a pleasure-driven culture. We are constantly told to do what feels right, to follow our hearts. The tenets of the popular culture are reinforced over and over again. We have gotten away from the painful, difficult decisions of discerning what is right, and then acting on them. That is not to say that people don't believe in right and wrong. If you took a survey and asked individuals: "Do you believe there is right and wrong," very few people would say, "No, I don't believe there is a right and a wrong." Of course they would say there is a right and a wrong. The problem is they make the truth relative, and they behave as if there is no absolute right and wrong. They don't act out their stated beliefs; they don't live them out in their own lives and, more important, they don't live them out with respect to other people's lives, including their own children. What are the consequences of a culture without truth? Without a shared belief system that is held and enforced, a culture disintegrates into moral chaos.

And who gets hurt the most when we lose truth? The poor. Why so many gated communities? To protect the rich from the moral chaos they have bequeathed to the rest of society. Wealthy middle-aged liberals talk a good game about "doing whatever feels good," and they surely followed their professors' advice and gave it a try when they were in college. But the reason their own lives aren't a train wreck is that, for the most part, they practice the Main Street values they profess to despise. The institution of marriage hasn't collapsed for them as it has for the poor, who took their lie about sex without consequences as gospel. Likewise, despite what you might read about the lives of the rich and famous in the supermarket tabloids, the top 20 percent of income earners have relatively low levels of divorce, out-of-wedlock births, and drug and alcohol use. The typical sixty-year-old upper-middle-class liberal did the sex-and-drugs-and-rock-and-roll thing when he was young, but today his own life looks more like *Leave It to Beaver* than *Modern Family*.

―――――

If our education system is going to give children the tools to be good, then there will have to be major changes. But it would be foolish to expect the system to fix itself. The good news is that we don't have to wait for politicians and stubborn teachers' unions. We can start the reform ourselves—family by family.

The first step is to recognize that expecting the federal or even state governments to run our local schools is a bad idea. The system of compulsory public education in America is a relic of the industrialization that swept the country at the end of the nineteenth century. At the same time people were leaving the farm to work in factories and on assembly lines to mass-produce Model Ts, they left the locally run one-room schoolhouse for education factories that mass-produced citizens in conformity to state rules. The assembly line and Model T were wonderful innovations in their time, but Ford only survived by transforming their assembly line and products to reflect both consumer demand and competitive challenges. Imagine a Ford showroom today with one model in one color that gets twelve miles per gallon and is equipped with an AM radio and an eight-track tape player. So why are we still mass-producing students in the educational factories we call schools?

The latest educational "reform"—the Common Core State Standards, which are sweeping the country—is just a revised version of mass-produced education. The Common Core is an attempt to impose on the entire country a single vision of "what students are expected to learn, so teachers and parents know what they need to do to help them."[2] And who determines "what students are expected to learn"? The same bureaucrats and ideologues who have already debased public education. Parents who believe their children should be taught to love the good, the true, and the beautiful should be very skeptical of the promises of Common Core.

Government is the problem here. Bureaucracies don't care about the customer; they are focused on making and following rules. Success is determined by whether the process was strictly followed, not by the result. Don't you think it's time we bring our schools into the twenty-first century and liberate educators from the antiquated rules that treat our children like a Model T?

Karen and I have seven children, and we can tell you that each one has different interests, different needs, and different ways of learning. They are all bright and curious and full of potential. But if they all went through the same public school, you'd see wildly different results. Committed parents know better than any bureaucrat what is best for their children. Now we're doing well enough to send them to good Catholic schools. Early in our marriage, however, that was not an option, so we dedicated the time necessary to teach them at home. Karen bore most of the burden, and it certainly was not easy, but the reward came when we saw our kids flourishing under the individual attention and personalized curricula. I know home-schooling is not for everyone; starting out, we didn't think it would be for us. But today there is a thriving homeschool com-munity, with parents cooperating in neighborhoods or linked into internet homeschool programs. For many, homeschooling can be an excellent, low-cost option for educating your kids.

———

Public schools are "free"—paid for by your tax dollars—but the results they deliver can vary widely. One in four American children drops out of school before graduating.[3] Obviously that dropout rate is not spread evenly across all American communities. In towns like Murray's Belmont—think Palo Alto, Brookline, or Bethesda—it's not one in four; it's more like one in forty. But in working-class Fishtown—communities like Saginaw, East St. Louis, and the Bronx—the rate is much higher. The odds are stacked against these kids. Most of them come from poor families with one parent in the home. The pop culture they imbibe promotes all the wrong things—and the local community feels more like a war zone than a neighborhood.

When I was a senator, I met with a small group of seniors who were the only college-bound students at William Penn High School, a large inner-city school in North Philadelphia. They had just been told by an Ivy League college recruiter that given their race, income, and academic record, almost any college would take them for free. I asked these students, "What is the biggest challenge you face to realize your dreams?" Silence, heads down. Then a young man in the back haltingly raised his hand—"Getting to school alive every day," he said. There was not even any nervous laughter, just continued silence. When I asked if everyone agreed, all of their heads nodded. Upon further questioning they explained the threat was not street criminals but their envious classmates at William Penn.

The Fishtown kids fail in disproportionate numbers. But we have to ask, aren't we the ones failing them? The answer is not to pour billions more into the federal Department of Education. The answer is a revolution in education that begins in the home.

—————

I often ask parents, "Who is the customer of the education system?" The answer I almost always get is "Our children." To which I reply, "Wrong!"

Then I ask, "Who is responsible for the education of your child, you or the school?" The light goes on as parents recognize that they, not the school, are responsible for their child's education. Therefore *they* are the customers, and the school's job is to help them provide an educational setting that will maximize their child's potential.

We have allowed the education establishment to convince us that we parents are simply not capable of overseeing our own children's education—that we need trained professionals to decide what is best for our children. But who knows your children better, you or the superintendent? Who was your child's first teacher, you or the superintendent? Whose singular concern is the best interest of your child, yours or the superintendent's? Who loves your child the most, you or the superintendent? Actually, no one in the government-run school system is focused on the best learning environment for *your* child. Not that there aren't well-meaning, wonderful people in the system; it's just not their job. Like everyone else in government, they are overwhelmed with process—filling out forms to show they are complying with federal and state mandates.

If the first step to reform is encouraging parents to take command of their kids' education and not delegate it to the government, the second step is to break the stranglehold of the teachers' unions on public education. Unions were once an important part of the industrial economy, and they protected workers from unreasonable conditions and demands

and ensured basic safety in factories. My coal miner grandfather was the treasurer of his mine workers' local and a union
man through and through. In those days, there were few laws
to protect workers, and the conditions he had to endure in the
mines because immigrant labor was cheap and expendable
were really tough. Thankfully, those days are gone, but I still
support the right of private sector workers to organize and
negotiate wages and working conditions.

But teachers' unions, in the name of protecting their members, are often the biggest obstacles to reforming our schools
for the benefit of both teachers and students. Part of the problem is collective bargaining. Federal employee unions are
barred from collective bargaining and using union dues for
political purposes. Many teachers' unions have no such
restrictions. They use the power of collective bargaining to
richly fund the union's political operation. They use that
machine to elect school board members who pay back the
unions with pay raises while blocking efforts to remove
incompetent teachers, to institute merit-based pay, and to
expand school choice.

The link is pretty clear. Our schools as a whole are doing
poorly, but school systems with collective bargaining tend to
do far worse. For example, according to the National Assess-
ment of Educational Progress, in 2011 only 40 percent of
fourth-grade students performed at or above their grade level
in math, and a mere 32 percent performed at or above their
grade level in reading.[4] But consider this: in Chicago, which

permits collective bargaining by teachers' unions, students are barely halfway to the national average, with only 20 percent of students at grade level in math and only 18 percent at grade level in reading. Meanwhile, Charlotte, North Carolina, a large urban school district, prohibits collective bargaining. Charlotte's students are beating the national average, with 48 percent proficiency in math and 36 percent in reading, besting the Chicago students by 28 and 18 points, respectively. You'll find similar disparities between New York City, where there is collective bargaining, and Austin, Texas, where there isn't.[5] Most of us take the commonsense view that schools should be focused on student and teacher performance. But the teachers' unions are often opposed to that commonsense goal.

It is easy to lay the blame on an antiquated education model, but that model worked much better when I was in grade school. It is failing now in part because it is being called on to do so much more. I have yet to meet a teacher that didn't tell me that family is the most important determinant of success in the classroom. Too many children arrive at school unprepared to learn or with serious behavioral issues or both. Of course, the president's idea is taking kids out of the home and putting them into a government-structured day care program instead of trying to address the root cause, broken families.

———

It's extremely important that our children's education at home and in school equip them with the basic skills they will need in their career. Parents are right to be concerned about the kind of character being formed in our public schools, but the foundation of character, like the foundation for learning, is built at home. Karen and I thought this was so important for our children that we searched for tools to help us impart those virtues to them. She ended up writing a book, *Everyday Graces: A Child's Book of Good Manners*, which, along with Bill Bennett's *The Book of Virtues*, became our homeschool curriculum on character formation.

Every child who goes through twelve years of public schooling should have what he needs to be a good citizen and to take part in the working life of this country. Not everyone has the aptitude or can afford to go to a four-year college. For many kids, a job or vocational training is the better option. All kids are different, and if one of mine decided to become the best auto mechanic in the country, that would be fine by me. I'm not requiring my kids to go to Penn State (though they do have to be Nittany Lions fans). And I'd much rather my children know how to fix an eighteen-wheeler or enlist in the navy than spend $150,000 to marinate for four years in the toxic ideology of academia while never missing a weekend party.

―――

When politicians talk about the need for a better-educated workforce, they generally follow that up with talks about increasing Stafford Loans and Pell Grants for kids going to college.[6] But what about the 70 percent I have been talking about who won't graduate from college? What about the unglamorous task of making sure that the next generation of American workers have the education and training they need to succeed by using their minds *and* their hands?

I think the answer is found in institutions and programs such as the Latin Builders Association Academy, a charter high school for construction and business management in Miami, Florida. We need more places like LBA Academy, which is the first charter school in the country started by a business association. The goal for the students at the LBA Academy upon graduation is to continue to college, then work for a member company in a well-paying job or start their own business. And the association members mentor and guide the students. It's a ground-up, community-based approach to providing real skills and experience to students who need these kinds of options.

Career and technical education (CTE) like this equips secondary, postsecondary, and adult students with the skills for high-paying jobs. With roots going back to the Civil War, CTE is the tried and true way to help young people be competitive in the workforce. It's the best way to train students for good blue collar jobs, and industries such as health science and manufacturing desperately need skilled laborers. In fact, when unemployment was at its worst in the Great Recession, there were half a million open jobs in transportation and utilities, and a quarter million in manufacturing, to name just a couple of sectors.[7]

Right now, approximately twelve million students are in secondary and postsecondary CTE programs across the nation. Both federal and state policies should support access to robust CTE programs as we look for creative ways to encourage workforce readiness. For instance, how about encouraging or even creating incentives for business associations to sponsor charter schools like LBA Academy? And as a way to help finance charter schools, how about expanding tax-free education savings accounts that could be started at birth and funded by friends, families, or businesses to help pay the tuition for charter or private schools?

———

As I traveled across the country in 2011 and 2012, I visited countless communities and schools to develop a plan to revitalize our economy. I did not visit the Harvards and Yales of America—their voices are heard in Washington every day. Instead, I visited institutions like Kirkwood Community College outside Cedar Rapids, Iowa, where they are actually training students for real jobs. I talked to the administrators at Kirkwood about my plan for increasing manufacturing jobs by having businesses and schools like Kirkwood work together on job training. Unbeknownst to me, the hotel where I stayed was staffed by Kirkwood students learning about the hospitality business. They were as professional as any staff I've come across in a Marriott or a Hilton. I later learned that the hotel had even earned the "Four Diamond Award" for its services and amenities. Practical instruction like this might not confer Ivy League prestige on its students, but schools like Kirkwood can play a vital role in helping kids make the transition from finishing high school to getting a job and all that entails—becoming a productive part of the community, getting on a career ladder, and eventually getting married and starting a family.

Education reform should begin with the family. Let's empower parents to give their children the keys to success and then give them the choice of the school that is the best setting for them to live their American Dream. A century ago, Republicans took pride in breaking up corporate monopolies. Now it's time to end the near-monopoly of government-run public schools.

CHAPTER NINE

GIVING THE AMERICAN WORKER A FIGHTING CHANCE

James Harrison grew up in the shadow of an aluminum manufacturing plant in northeastern Ohio. When he was born, in 1964, the plant employed his father and more than five hundred others, and the business was booming. Since the end of World War II, the company had experienced tremendous demand from around the world, and it ran three shifts to keep up. There was a job in the factory for anyone who had finished high school and was willing to work hard. After a few years on the job, the pay was enough to buy a home in town and comfortably provide for a family.

The owner of the company became quite wealthy but always lived in the town, attended a local church, and sat in the stands at the high school football games. He knew most of his employees by name and never missed the company's summer picnic.

The company did well throughout the 1960s and 1970s. Though growth had slowed somewhat by 1981, when James finished school and went to work there, it was still the same company he had known as a kid. By the late 1980s, however, competition from overseas was taking a toll, and the company was hiring fewer and fewer people. By 1990, the factory was no longer viewed as a good, reliable employer for local young men and women graduating from high school. Its export market had disappeared, and more of the company's domestic customers were choosing the more affordable products of offshore manufacturers.

In 1995, the company was sold to some out-of-town investors who had purchased similar businesses and thought they could run them more profitably. The new owners froze wages, cut benefits, and laid off 20 percent of the workforce. James hung on to his job, but it was a different place. Everyone anxiously waited for the other shoe to drop. Orders continued to decrease, and the factory was down to just one shift. In 1996, the company picnic was canceled to save money.

James and Susan had their first child, Jason, in 1997, and Thomas was born in 1999. In 2004, the aluminum company's owner filed for Chapter 13 bankruptcy and laid off many more employees. The company never recovered, and one day in late 2008, as the Great Recession set in, James showed up to find the factory doors locked and the lights off. The company had gone into Chapter 7 bankruptcy, and its assets were being liquidated. James had been earning $22.50 an hour with a company-provided health insurance plan. Now it was all gone.

There weren't many other careers for which James was qualified. Acquiring a new set of skills would be expensive, and he felt a little old for that anyway. After a feverish search, he took a job at a home-improvement store thirty miles away. The pay was just $12.50 an hour, with no benefits in the first year. Five years later he's still there, making $14.25 an hour. Susan works as a nurse at an elementary school, and the two incomes are just enough to get by. They have cut back where they can—summer trips to the lake, dinners out, gym memberships, and contributions to their retirement plans. There's nothing set aside for the boys' college, and the idea of ever retiring seems like a joke.

The once-proud factory town where the Harrisons live is littered with home foreclosures. Financial stress has weakened marriages, and many families are falling apart. Social problems that James and Susan hardly knew about when they were growing up—drug abuse, domestic violence, out-of-wedlock pregnancy—are commonplace now.

=====

The factory towns in western Pennsylvania that I represented in Congress in the early 1990s were filled with thousands of families like the Harrisons. Those people have been forced into lower-paying service jobs, or they have to make the long commute to Pittsburgh for work.

Nearly nine million jobs have been lost since the beginning of the Great Recession.[1] For some, it seems like American economic decline is the inevitable new reality that we'll have to get used to. I don't believe it. When I was in Congress, I was told that the jobs Pennsylvania had lost weren't coming back. And guess what—that was wrong. Yes, Pittsburgh's mills are gone, but their places have been taken by office parks, high-tech manufacturers, and, of course, Walmarts, Cinemark Theatres, and Home Depots. The report of Pittsburgh's death was an exaggeration. But what about the little towns built around one factory, or the rural areas that lived on mining or timber? In the small cities and towns of the Rust Belt, people had started to accept the inevitability of decline, but something has happened to change that. Now many rural areas are witnessing growth, and it is spreading to the cities. What happened?

That boom is coming from oil and gas development, made possible by hydraulic fracturing ("fracking"), which releases oil and natural gas from shale rock formations. It turns out that the United States is the Saudi Arabia of shale rock. Fracking has filled North Dakota with good-paying jobs and reduced the state's unemployment rate to 2.6 percent.[2] North Dakota shouldn't be alone. There are substantial deposits of shale oil and gas in the Rust Belt states of West Virginia, New York, Michigan, Pennsylvania, and Ohio. Even President Obama has acknowledged that there is probably enough American natural gas, in deposits such as Pennsylvania's Marcellus Shale formation, to last us a hundred years.[3]

On the campaign trail in 2012, I met Dick Holcombe from rural Sullivan County in northeastern Pennsylvania, which is ground zero for Pennsylvania's shale gas boom. After traveling the world for his career in business, Dick returned home to Sullivan County to start an e-commerce services company. It has been successful and is now the largest private employer in the county. Dick could have gone anywhere, but two things drew him back home—caring for his aging parents and shale. He understood the potential of the fracking revolution for the region. As he puts it, he wanted to see what happens when a fifth-generation dairy farmer becomes a millionaire overnight. He got back to Sullivan County just in time—there have been plenty of millionaire dairy farmers to observe.

Many families he knew growing up, particularly the dairy farmers and small-mine operators, were land rich but cash poor. Families that had been scraping by for generations are now millionaires because of gas leases, and land values have risen beyond anyone's expectations. Fortunately, the values that saw these families through the tough times when manufacturing and farming were in decline are guiding them through the boom times now. Prudence and a sense of perspective are critical for families who have in effect won the lottery because of a gas lease.

Aside from the increased traffic on the county's scenic roads, not much has changed. Many dairymen are still farming. The small coal operators are still mining and finding additional uses for their equipment in the shale industry. What has changed is the return of a sense of value and purpose.

Most people thought that America had left places like Sullivan County behind. Dick Holcombe knew that wasn't true. America hasn't left Sullivan County behind, because Sullivan County *is* America.

———

Mahoning County, Ohio, where the Harrisons live, is atop the western end of the Utica Shale, a major new source of oil. Energy companies have now invested millions in evaluating the area and are planning to move aggressively into the region. As it did in North Dakota, shale oil could create an economic boom not only in the energy sector but in all the businesses that will grow or be created as workers and new residents flock to the area. The eastern Ohio economy, which has been a drag on the state for decades, could become the state's economic engine all because of oil.[4]

Shale oil and gas could transform the rural and Rust Belt regions where many of the deposits lie. You would think that reviving these communities and encouraging domestic energy production would be a national priority. Yet the Obama administration, incredibly enough, is trying to sideline the fracking revolution, which is providing abundant new sources of clean-burning, affordable natural gas. Most environmentalists didn't oppose natural gas ten years ago, when it was three times the price it is now. These liberals never want to see the words "affordable and plentiful" in the same sentence with "fossil fuels."

Obama's most notorious attack on the fossil fuel industry has been his refusal to permit the construction of the Keystone pipeline, which would transport oil from Canada and the Bakken Shale in North Dakota and create thousands of jobs.[5] But there have been numerous other decisions that have destroyed American jobs or shipped them overseas. His moratorium on oil production in the Gulf of Mexico after the BP oil spill turned into a "permatorium," according to the people I spoke with in Louisiana.[6] In spite of Obama's best efforts, oil and gas production is up, but only on lands owned by private citizens. It is down on government-owned land both on and off shore. This de facto moratorium is a triple whammy for the average American—fewer jobs, higher energy prices, and higher budget deficits because of lost revenue from drilling.

When so many Americans are hurting, why would a president act so irresponsibly? Because the Obama administration is filled with environmental extremists, "true believers" who are committed to the eventual elimination of fossil fuels no matter the human cost. And that cost is enormous. It's not just in the energy industry itself that jobs are at stake. Every business in the country is affected—from farming to high tech to manufacturing. Especially in manufacturing, where American workers are up against foreign competition, energy costs can determine whether jobs stay in America or go overseas. In many manufacturing industries, energy contributes over 15 percent of a product's cost.[7]

———

If restoring the American Dream is our goal, restoring our manufacturing industry must be an essential piece of the plan. Most American businesses have to compete against other American businesses. The government might make life difficult for them with excessive taxation and regulation, but at least the competition is up against the same thing. But manufacturers face foreign competitors that operate under different rules and with different costs. Many foreign manufacturers enjoy government subsidies and weak environmental and labor laws.

That is why I think we need to look at the manufacturing sector of the economy differently from other sectors. When it comes to foreign competition, our government has a legitimate role in laying down laws that even the playing field. For much of our history, American manufacturing was protected by tariffs. Today, many of our manufacturers lose business and jobs not because they are uncompetitive but because of misguided government regulations.

Most people assume that foreign manufacturers' biggest advantage is cheap labor. A study sponsored by the National Association of Manufacturers in 2003 attempted to quantify the competitive disadvantage of U.S. manufacturers against their top five competitors. The study considered all the major costs, including labor, energy, raw materials, taxes, regulations, and litigation. It determined that U.S. manufacturers had a 22 percent cost disadvantage *excluding* labor costs.[8] High wages are not costing us jobs. We're losing jobs because of high corporate tax rates, excessive regulatory burdens, and other anti-business policies coming from Washington.

Our single largest disadvantage is our corporate tax rate, the highest in the industrialized world. It's so high that even President Obama has considered trimming it. So let's reduce the corporate tax to a flat rate of 20 percent with no fancy deductions, no loopholes—just a 20 percent net income tax. But *reducing* taxes isn't enough; to create a boom in manufacturing jobs in the United States, we should *eliminate* the corporate tax for manufacturers. That will attract investment capital to American manufacturing plants, and capital creates jobs. If we could do only one thing to make our manufacturers more competitive, eliminating the corporate tax would be it.

Next should be regulatory reform. I have had small manufacturers from Missouri Valley, Iowa, to Tampa, Florida, tell me that the burden has gotten dramatically worse during the Obama years. The attitude of state and federal regulators is "We know best how to run your business." The burden is particularly heavy for small businesses, which create the most manufacturing jobs. Large corporations have compliance departments that can handle these regulations, but many small businesses find it nearly impossible. Many actually shut down because they can't bear the cost of compliance. In America, you shouldn't need an army of lawyers just so you can run a small manufacturing business. But that's what happens when we surrender power to the government and let it expand beyond its justifiable duty to set up and referee the ground rules that protect customers, employees, shareholders, and competition.

In its first two years, the Obama administration imposed seventy-five major regulations that cost businesses more than $38 billion. To that cost is added the additional taxpayer cost of paying for the ever-increasing army of regulators. It's time that regulations were subject to a serious cost-benefit analysis. For example, a new regulation from the Environmental Protection Agency on emissions from commercial boilers is estimated to add $1.8 billion in new annual compliance costs to companies and a one-time implementation fee of $5.2 billion—with negligible benefits.[9] Tell me: What's the point of that, except to use the power of regulation to destroy private business?

This is not an uncommon situation. In pursuit of minuscule health benefits, the Obama administration has heaped enormous costs on manufacturers. Everyone loses. American plants can't comply with all these new standards and still make a profit, so they close. We lose jobs and tax revenue, and government will likely have to pay unemployment and other benefits to laid-off workers, whose communities and families will suffer. And as for the environmental benefit—there is none. Because these products are now being made in countries with lax environmental laws and the goods will have to be transported long distances back to the United States, there will actually be more harmful pollutants released. This is insanity! We need to analyze *real* costs and *real* benefits, tailoring the regulations to minimize costs for the maximum achievable benefits.

Over the years, American manufacturers have opened up factories all over the world for a variety of different reasons. Some factories were opened to serve markets in that country that couldn't be competitively served from here. Some companies outsourced only certain parts or assemblies to keep the rest of the domestic manufacturing competitive and therefore keep some jobs here. Other companies have packed up completely.

Whatever the motivation, American companies have made billions of dollars in profits overseas. Those profits are taxed by the country where they are made. The remainder is sitting in the companies' foreign subsidiaries instead of being repatriated to America. The reason? Taxes, of course. There is a 35 percent tax on all money brought back to America. The argument for the tax is that it is both an incentive and a punishment. It's an incentive to keep manufacturing here, and a punishment if the company doesn't keep it here. But who is getting hurt? There are legitimate reasons for companies to move production to other countries. Some countries, for example, require certain products sold in their country to be made there; others impose tariffs that make it impossible to manufacture a product in the United States and ship to those countries. In fact, most of the offshore manufacturing is not a result of making a bigger profit for the company, it is about survival. Our tax laws shouldn't be punishing American companies, because it ends up hurting America and our workers.

Apple keeps over a billion dollars of foreign profits in a fund that invests that money overseas. What if Apple had an incentive to repatriate that money to the United States and invest it in domestic manufacturing? Taxation of manufacturers' overseas profits should not encourage them to keep the money in foreign bank accounts or invested in overseas competitors. It should encourage them to bring those profits back home, where they can be invested in new plants and equipment or pay dividends to shareholders.

Although we should move to a flat corporate income tax, there is one corporate tax credit that I would keep in place. That's the research and development tax credit, which is necessary to keep American manufacturing ahead of the curve. I would double it and make it permanent. Our tax laws should encourage companies to invest in the future. Burdensome regulation and tax laws do just the reverse, encouraging short-term thinking about profits to cover the costs of the regulations and taxes.

Finally, we need to examine our trade policies. I am a free trader, but we have to look at the effect of free trade on the average person. Importing lower-cost goods can benefit lower-income people and the average consumer. Just about everybody loves the prices at Walmart, for example. But as with regulations, we need to assess that benefit in light of its costs. Are importers following the same rules that govern domestic manufacturers? Are existing trade laws fair and properly enforced? When we make policy, we should always think about the people it affects, like, for instance, the people I met in Bemidji, Minnesota, during the 2012 presidential campaign.

———

Bemidji is a town of about fourteen thousand of the friendliest and hardest-working people you could ever hope to meet. It's the home of the famous oversized statues of Paul Bunyan and his faithful blue ox, Babe. Built in 1937 for the local winter carnival and designed only to last a year or two, the statues achieved national prominence after they were featured in *Life* magazine.

When I visited Bemidji, it was abundantly clear to me that it is a special place. Places like Bemidji may be small, seemingly inconsequential dots on a map. But when you add them all up, their influence on our economy and culture is enormous. These towns make our country exceptional. What brought me to Bemidji were sweater vests.

In politics, many of the things done by candidates are staged for a purpose. Candidates can get pretty calculating about everything from their hairstyle to the shoes they wear. My sweater vests, however, were not part of any premeditated strategy. It just so happened that on a cold December night in Iowa, I wore a sweater vest under my sport coat to keep warm. I don't like wearing overcoats, and I like to pack light (vests are less bulky than sweaters or heavy coats). I was the last of the presidential candidates to speak at an event hosted by Mike Huckabee, and by the time it was my turn, the auditorium in Des Moines had gotten a little warm. My speech, to an audience of committed conservatives, was a big success. Some reporter happened to joke on Twitter that it must have been the sweater vest. The rest, as the saying goes, is history!

At a time when voters were looking for a down-to-earth, sensible alternative to President Obama—someone who reflected their values and perspective—the sweater vest became a symbol of "Middle America" in contrast to the muddle-headed elitism of the Obama administration. Obama is famously "cool"—so cool that you can't imagine him in a sweater vest. But a lot of Americans were fed up with his indifference to them, and the lowly sweater vest became their symbol.

After that speech in Iowa, people started asking our campaign for a Santorum sweater vest. With my focus on reviving manufacturing, I decided that if we were going to offer sweater vests, they better be made in America. Easier said than done. It proved remarkably difficult to find a manufacturer that could supply a sweater vest that was truly and completely "made in the USA" in the quantities demanded. Eventually we found a manufacturer in Bemidji, Minnesota, and that's where Bill Batchelder comes into our story.

Bemidji Woolen Mills started when Bill's great-grandfather was sawing railroad ties for underground mines. In his hardscrabble life, he managed to pull together enough money to start a potato warehouse. Later, realizing that every town needed a woolen mill to make clothing and that Bemidji, where winters are as harsh as anywhere in the continental United States, didn't have one, he turned his potato warehouse into a woolen mill. When the Chevy factory closed down in 1929, at the onset of the Great Depression, Bill's great-grandfather purchased the factory, despite everybody's warning that it was a bad idea. He wanted to move the woolen mill into a larger space, and the factory seemed perfect. At the start of World War II, he won a contract to produce army blankets.

When the postwar baby boom reached its peak, family station wagons crisscrossed the country, stopping to see Paul Bunyan and Babe. That's when the woolen mill hit its stride. Kids and families wanted clothes that reminded them of America's pioneers and lumberjacks, clothes made by Bemidji Woolen Mills.

One of the highlights of the campaign was visiting the workers at Bemidji Woolen Mills, where they turned out our sweater vests by the hundreds. I then walked two blocks down the street to the embroidery shop to see the campaign logo stitched on.

Bill told me policy makers just don't understand how Main Street works, what creates jobs and sustains communities. He mentioned a Democrat in the Minnesota senate who had proposed a tax on clothing priced over a hundred dollars. Presumably the point was to soak the people who can afford such clothing. But in fact it punishes the worker who makes that clothing. Taxes like that make it harder for small businesses to survive and create jobs.

It's not being sentimental to say that Bemidji is the kind of "sweater vest" town that is the heart and soul of America. It's a scandal that the concerns of people who live in places like Bemidji—their hopes and dreams, their jobs, their families— get short shrift from politicians of both parties. Towns like Bemidji just don't fit into their plans or their vision for the future. We should stand up for places like Bemidji and for the blue collar conservative values they represent.

CHAPTER TEN

RAISING HOPE
INSTEAD
OF TAXES

We can argue about the proper breadth and strength of the safety net that the federal government stretches beneath its citizens—whether to extend unemployment benefits or guarantee health insurance, for instance. But two components of the safety net, Social Security and Medicare, are so well established and relied on by so many that the debate is only about *how*, not *whether*, to fund them. That's a debate we've got to settle soon, because both programs are headed for a financial cliff, and that's when the seniors who are just making ends meet get hurt—badly.

Apart from entitlements, the federal government most directly affects Americans' household finances through the tax system. Here too the status quo is a mess. The tax code is a mix of needless complexity and perverse incentives. We need a system that is simple and logical. It should promote behavior that builds strong families, businesses, and communities.

It has been years, unfortunately, since Democrats and Republicans had a productive discussion about reforming Social Security, Medicare, and the tax code. Washington's paralysis is imperiling the American Dream, and a lot of voters are ready to reach for their pitchforks.

Social Security is often called the "third rail" of American politics. In other words, "Touch it and you die politically."[1] Politician after politician has run from the problems that appear when you shine light on the Social Security program. And it's no secret why. Americans cherish the program. We've all paid into it. Many see it as a safety net for their retirement—if they can ever afford to retire. And many older Americans count on it. But the hard reality is that Social Security pays out more in benefits than it receives in taxes. Social Security had been a pay-as-you-go system, with current taxpayers contributing at least enough to meet current benefits. But that ended in 2011.[2]

Some politicians have convinced a willing public that a Social Security "trust fund" finances their benefits. That is true in theory but false in practice. The trust fund is a drawer full of IOUs requiring the federal government to pay back the money it borrowed over the years when Social Security taxes exceeded the amount needed to pay benefits. Of course, the federal government already spends more money than it takes in, not counting Social Security, so when the Social Security Administration submits an IOU, the federal government simply borrows more money and issues a new IOU to pay Social Security benefits.

In 2013, Social Security was projected to spend $75 billion more on benefits than it received in taxes.[3] With the baby boom generation becoming eligible for benefits, that number is expected to more than double in ten years. We can't continue to do what Washington's pathetic political class has done for twenty years and leave this problem to the next generation of politicians to handle. The longer we wait, the more sudden and painful the changes will be and the more those who can't afford it will get hurt. For example, according to estimates, Social Security IOUs will be paid off in nineteen years. If no action is taken, the law requires an automatic 25 percent cut in benefits for every senior to keep the program solvent. I understand that Social Security is not like other entitlements—its recipients, unlike people on welfare, have been paying taxes into the system for years. They feel, quite understandably, that Social Security is simply paying them *their* money. But make no mistake, changes will have to be made and fairly soon. We need to have a rational discussion so we all understand the scale of the problem and the options to solve it. We must make the right choices and make them before the program hits the wall.

There are a number of ways we can do this. In the 1990s, when I was in the U.S. Senate, I supported personal retirement accounts as a long-term fix. This approach would give younger workers the opportunity to do better than they would in the current underfunded system.[4] I still believe that a 401(k) approach to Social Security would provide better benefits for most seniors and is the most financially responsible way of solving the problem. The problem is that the current system is so underfunded that we need to get it on stable footing for current and near-term retirees before we look too far into the future.

So how do we do that when increasing payroll taxes will cause increased unemployment and slow economic growth, and decreasing benefits could harm those whom the program is designed for, the elderly and disabled? Why don't we first see if any benefits are going to people who don't meet the criteria of being old and disabled?

Social Security was established in 1936, when life expectancy was sixty-one. Benefits were set as follows: early old-age benefits were available at sixty-two, with full old-age benefits available at sixty-five. Today, average life expectancy is seventy-nine, so one might assume that early old-age benefits would begin at eighty and full old-age benefits at eighty-three. That's not the case, of course, although in 1983 a Democratic

Congress and a Republican president agreed to gradually raise the full-eligibility age to sixty-seven by 2027. The most important step we can take is to recognize in law what people already know to be true. Sixty-two in America today is not old. Tell a sixty-two-year-old that he's "past his prime" and see what reaction you get—you might need to duck. Yet that same sixty-two-year-old has no problem signing up for "old-age" benefits under Social Security; in fact, more than 70 percent do. Starting benefits this early would be fine if the system were solvent, but we don't have the money. The system is running in the red, and it is getting worse every year.

It might make sense to gradually reform the system over the next thirty-six years by increasing the eligibility for early retirement by one month every year. Once early eligibility reaches sixty-five in 2052, further increases would be tied to increases in life expectancy. I propose doing something similar for the normal eligibility age—start raising it in 2028 until it reaches sixty-nine in 2052. For everyone born after 1983, I would tie both eligibility ages to increases in life expectancy, so every subsequent generation would receive benefits for the same number of years as the previous. I would do the same for Medicare, raising the eligibility age by one month per year until it reaches sixty-nine in 2052.

There is another big difference between seniors in 1936 and seniors today—wealth. In the 1930s the poorest age group of adults was people over sixty-five. Today the wealthiest age group is people over sixty-five. In part that's because Social

Security and Medicare provide them with a minimum level of income and healthcare coverage, but it is mostly because many "young" seniors continue to work and because so many in this generation have lived the American Dream of opportunity and success. Who, by the way, are the poorest age group? Eighteen- to thirty-year-olds.[5]

Some have suggested raising taxes to pay for the shortfall in Social Security. In other words, they would increase taxes on poor grandchildren to pay wealthy grandparents. You say not all seniors are wealthy—true, so let's begin with reducing the scheduled cost-of-living increases in benefits to the wealthy recipients who don't need them.

There is even a benefit that we could eliminate without controversy. We should stop paying Social Security benefits to dependents (children under eighteen) of wealthy Social Security recipients. This usually occurs when wealthy men over fifty marry and have children.

There are dozens of other reasonable benefit changes that we ought to discuss. The most important thing is for the American public and seniors to have this discussion with a clear idea of the magnitude of the problem and what we want to accomplish—bridging the funding gap without hurting lower-income workers, lower-income seniors, or the overall economy.

———

Compared with Medicare, Social Security is in decent shape. It can survive with modest adjustments that will affect only the wealthiest and healthiest seniors, but Medicare is a different story.

Medicare was started in 1965 to provide seniors with a basic level of healthcare, just as Social Security was to provide seniors with a basic level of income. The cost to the taxpayer of providing Social Security benefits increases with inflation and population. The cost of Medicare likewise increases with population and inflation, but also with innovation. Think of all of the procedures, treatments, knowledge, drugs, and devices that improve the quality and length of life, and then think of how much more those cost. Then think of how much more is in the pipeline and how much longer we can extend life.

This is a great problem to have, but there's no solution to it under the Medicare model that was designed fifty years ago. Some of the problems of Medicare are similar to the problems of Obamacare—in both cases the government is far too involved in dictating terms and prices. This meddling inevitably deprives customers of choice, creates costly inefficiency, and discourages innovation. Even before the passage of Obamacare, more than half of the money spent on healthcare in America was paid for by either the federal or state governments.[6] Under Obamacare, the federal government in particular calls the shots for reimbursements and covered procedures, as well as policies on privacy, billing, competition, and a whole host of other details. A true revolution in affordable, quality healthcare will not come from more government interference, as we have with Obamacare, but from letting the healthcare system benefit from competition, just as telecommunications and other high-tech industries do.

I have supported this approach for decades. In fact, when I was in the Senate I worked to make Medicare Part D, the drug benefit offered to seniors, adhere to market principles. Until President Obama tinkered with it in Obamacare, Part D was the first entitlement program in history to spend less money than the budget experts predicted. So far, Part D, which is privately run but partially funded by the government with some federal oversight, is coming in about $340 billion *under* its ten-year budget. Medicare, which is completely funded and administered by the government, is expected to double its spending to *$1.1 trillion* over the next decade.[7] Let's use the example of Part D and the popular Medicare Advantage option to create a dynamic public-private partnership that will improve the efficiency, quality, and affordability of the Medicare program.

———

Social Security and Medicare face primarily demographic challenges, but the bad economy of the Obama years has caused another entitlement program to explode. Spending on food stamps doubled between 2006 and 2012. We have to put food stamps recipients on the path to success. That means work. The great success of the 1996 Welfare Reform Act was its work requirement. We never applied that requirement to food stamps, and that was a mistake. We should, in fact, make it a rule that all federal benefits programs that go to able-bodied Americans have a work requirement.

Of course, some Americans are seriously disabled and will never be entirely self-sufficient. I'm the father of a child with disabilities, and I know how difficult that can be. But unfortunately, we've also seen an explosion of fraudulent disability claims in order to tap benefits from the Supplemental Security Income (SSI) and Social Security Disability Income (SSDI) programs. The amount of money wasted because of this abuse is substantial. Between 2009 and 2012, more than 5.9 million people were added to the SSDI program. That's more than twice the number of new jobs that were created in the same period. Unfortunately, when the economy is hurting, people become "creative" to secure resources for themselves and their families. Another word for creative is fraudulent.[8]

When I was in office, I was bombarded with stories of children's being coached to lie by parents hoping to get money from SSI, or disaffected workers' claiming SSDI as unemployment benefits were about to end. Such fraud not only steals from the taxpayers, it helps bankrupt a system that should be focused on serving the truly needy and disabled.

Thomas Jefferson articulated a principle that should guide a free society as it considers how to help its needy and vulnerable members: "What more is necessary to make us a happy and prosperous people? ... [A] wise and frugal government ... which shall leave [men] free to regulate their own pursuits of industry and improvement, and shall not take from the mouth of labor the bread it has earned."[9]

We need to get back to the basic functions of government. And investing in our national infrastructure—our bridges, rails, highways, and dams—is something all conservatives can agree is one of the things government must do well. But we need dramatic reforms to reduce the cost of public infrastructure, starting with renegotiating many union contracts. And we need sufficient revenues at all levels of government, especially at the state and local levels, for this investment to bring an end to the massive infrastructure deficit we have. Government needs to get out of some of the areas it shouldn't be in, like certain entitlements, and redirect resources to infrastructure. This investment will create jobs and strengthen the foundation of our national economy.

———

While we should be leery of grand government schemes like Obamacare, we must remember that government can be a force for good, and it is in our interest that it be healthy and functional. The mind-blowing waste of Obama's "stimulus," which lined the pockets of the administration's cronies but did little for the economy, has left many citizens with an understandably dim view of their federal government. But Michael Gerson and Peter Wehner, presidential advisors in the George W. Bush administration, insist that excessive cynicism about the government is dangerous: "The reputation of government is an important national asset—and an irreplaceable source of national pride. Government overreach by the Left has degraded that asset. Today's hemorrhaging of trust in public institutions, if left to run its course, will only further degrade it. Skepticism toward government is one thing; outright hostility is injurious to the health of American democracy itself. How can citizens be expected to love their country if they are encouraged to hold its government in utter contempt?"[10]

Conservatives understand this best when it comes to national defense. That is a part of the national government that seems "conservative," especially for blue collar conservatives. Because it embodies the values of patriotism, honor, and sacrifice, the military is the part of the federal government we're proud of. It reflects what is best in our country.

Military spending, moreover, is generally more productive than other government spending. Yes, the Pentagon can waste money with the best of them (Senator Tom Coburn of Oklahoma has called it the "Department of Everything" and identified nearly $70 billion that could be cut over ten years without affecting national security).[11] But defense spending supports manufacturing jobs in shipbuilding and aerospace, drives high-tech research and development, and most important, of course, defends our country and our national interests.

President Obama's hostility to military culture is no secret. Not only does he seek to undermine that culture by imposing a politically correct social agenda on our forces, but he is making the fiscal crisis for which he bears so much responsibility an excuse to eviscerate the military, proposing massive cuts to manpower and weapons systems.[12] This is cutting meat, not fat. No one should be fooled by this opportunistic show of fiscal discipline.

————

The primary way that the government takes bread from the mouth of labor is taxation, and the federal tax system is a disgrace. It is confusing, conflicting, and confounding, and lately the Obama White House has wielded it as a weapon against its political opponents. Thanks to the dramatic growth and complexity of our tax system, the Internal Revenue Service is a uniquely effective tool to strike terror into political opponents. Unlike a legal probe by the Justice Department or another federal agency, an IRS accusation imposes on its target the presumption of guilt. A system that encourages such abuse should be condemned and demolished. A complete overhaul would allow us to reassess what types of activities the federal government should tax and how to best do it.

Let's look at the issue of what we should be taxing. Work is the key to success. It is so good for us that you might expect the government to encourage it. Well it doesn't. If we want people to work, we should stop taxing their wages. Let's develop a tax system where you get to keep everything you have worked for.

Rather than taxing working or giving, let's tax spending. Most of the world does just that, raising government revenues primarily from a sales or value-added tax. The main argument against a consumption tax is that it is harder on lower-income people. For example, a man with a wife and two kids earning $35,000 last year is likely to have spent all of it to provide for his family, whereas a family of four whose income is a million dollars has plenty to spare. So the lower-income family is paying a higher percentage of its income in taxes than the rich. That would be a reversal of the current progressive system of income tax, and it's a legitimate concern. One proposal for ameliorating the regressive nature of a consumption tax is called Fair Tax. I haven't endorsed it, but there is much to commend it as a starting point for the discussion of incentivizing working, saving, and giving while discouraging overconsumption.[13]

Enacting this kind of fundamental change to our tax system will require a presidential campaign and a national debate. So let's set the long-term overhaul aside and consider how we could mend some of the worst flaws in the current system.

A tax code can encourage certain behavior and punish other behavior. In addition to punishing work, ours punishes marriage. Since marriage is a critical factor in avoiding poverty, the tax code should encourage it. Removing the "marriage penalty" from the code is a good start, but we ought to go further and establish more tax benefits for married couples.

The most important act of stewardship for our country is raising the next generation of Americans. That next generation is, literally, the future of America. Low birthrates bespeak a lack of confidence and diminish our personal stake in the future. As we've seen in Europe, collapsing birthrates also make a welfare state unsustainable, as you inevitably end up with too few workers trying to support too many retirees. Karen and I are blessed with the responsibility of raising seven children. We have had no greater joy in our lives, but in the world today, it is also our greatest challenge. Let's set aside the cultural factors that I spoke of earlier and what they do to undermine a parent's ability to raise good, virtuous, faith-filled children. Let's look at how families with children are treated by the tax code.

There are a few provisions that lighten the tax burden on families with children, primarily the personal exemption—$3,900 in 2013 for you, your spouse, and all of your dependent children. That exemption reduces the amount of income subject to taxation. If this deduction had kept pace with inflation since 1969, it would be more than $6,000.

At the apex of the baby boom, the average American woman bore 3.5 children (and all those kids are now the ones retiring and receiving benefits). A typical family of four paid a total of 2 percent of its income to the federal government in taxes. Today the birthrate is less than 1.9 children per woman, and that same middle-income family of four (earning

$51,100) pays 9 percent of its income to the federal government. Even the refund that a family of four can obtain because of deductions is not enough to offset taxes paid to Social Security and Medicare. If you consider all of the state and local taxes that didn't exist in 1955, there is no question we are asking parents to do more with less in an environment in which it is much harder to raise children.

We should double the tax credits for children from $3,000 to $6,000 per child so that young couples can afford to raise a family.[14] That would put middle-income families back on a par, in terms of federal taxes, with their grandparents when they were having all of those kids in the 1950s.[15] Reducing taxes on families is the best investment government can make in our future. And to come full circle, it is the best investment we can make to ensure that programs like Social Security and Medicare live up to their promise to our nation's elderly.

―――

The economic policies of the Left not only are harming the poor, the low-skilled worker, and the entrepreneur, but as we all know they are hitting our pocketbook every day through the insidious creep of rising prices. The administration tells us that inflation is under control, but try convincing the mom who has seen chicken prices rise 16 percent, ground beef 18 percent, and bacon (my favorite) 22 percent. In survey after survey, Americans say they feel like they are falling behind, as their wages have stagnated and prices continue to rise on everything from food and energy to medical care and education. The principle culprit here is our central bank, the Federal Reserve. The activities of the Fed determine the cost of borrowing money by establishing interest rates for things like mortgages and car loans. Over the past few years, the Fed has been aggressively purchasing government debt, and in doing so driving interest rates down to nothing.

This is what's called "quantitative easing," and it has driven stock prices to all-time highs, to the delight of Wall Street. But putting all this additional money into circulation is driving up prices for Main Street. Many of the Wall Street economists who criticized my ideas about leveling the playing field for manufacturers so that low-skilled workers could find quality, family-sustaining jobs are cheering the intervention of the Federal Reserve to keep the good times rolling in the financial markets at the expense of those very workers.

When the economy begins to pick up steam, inflation will be an even greater problem for working families. I have serious doubts that the Fed will be able to unwind the problem it has created. That means even more price inflation in the future eroding purchasing power and pushing more and more people into the red.

———

The Harrisons are about fifteen years away from beginning to collect Social Security benefits—in about 2028, just about the time, if nothing is done, that the program will be able to pay only three-quarters of benefits due. No politician is talking about it, so the Harrisons are not aware of what is in store for them. They already feel as if they missed out on their town's economic good ol' days. Just wait till they find out what awaits them in retirement.

They are doing their part to fix the problem from the ground up, but they are relying on their leaders to attend to the top-down part.

CHAPTER ELEVEN

BELIEVING IN AMERICA'S FUTURE

James and Susan Harrison are optimistic people by nature. Though the last several years have been tough, they are grateful for the hand life has dealt them. They were born into strong, loving, supportive families in a safe town filled with decent, hardworking, community-minded people. While they are struggling financially, they still have their health, their faith, and two healthy, active sons. Not bad.

There are even signs that their financial situation is taking a turn for the better thanks to the Utica Shale they're sitting on top of. James has an interview for a job with a business that just came to the area to supply parts to the energy companies drilling for oil in eastern Ohio and western Pennsylvania. It pays well and has benefits. Susan has been spending more time helping her niece, who is single with a baby. Her niece is doing well in the nursing program she enrolled in, but it's a fragile situation and she needs lots of support. The boys are doing well, and it won't be long before they will have to think hard about what will happen after high school.

Like most Americans, they haven't paid a lot of attention to issues like the size of our national debt, rising food prices, or the problems with Medicare and Social Security. America has faced tougher challenges and has always come out fine. But the divisiveness in Washington is so unsettling that they no longer trust the president and Congress to do *anything*, much less the right thing.

America will bounce back, but we have our work cut out for us. For too many people, the American Dream seems unattainable. They've lost faith in the promise of hard and honest work. Others are pursuing a cheap counterfeit of the American Dream—a materialistic fantasy of riches, fame, and sex— that they absorb from movies and television and a hundred other channels of popular culture. We need leaders who will remind us what the real American Dream is—family, faith, freedom, opportunity, and service—not incite us to be envious of those who have achieved it. Above all, it's up to each

American family to adhere to the old adage, "Work as if everything depended on you, and pray as if everything depended on God."

━━━

This is not the first time America has faced a great challenge. There were times when our country faced a foreign threat and internal division, and we were saved by sacrifice on the battlefield. There were times of economic transformation—which always means disruption—when American enterprise surged to global leadership. In the present crisis, however, we risk abandoning the principles at the root of American greatness, the ideals set forth in the Declaration of Independence.

How is that happening? Have most Americans abandoned those ideals? Every poll in the last thirty years shows that roughly twice as many people identify themselves as "conservative" as identify themselves as "liberal." So why is our country moving to the left? For the same reason an undermanned, underfunded collection of colonists defeated the British Empire in the American Revolution—because they were willing to give their lives, their fortune, and their sacred honor for the cause. In short, the Left wants it more than we do. Barack Obama promised to "fundamentally transform" the United States, and his record in the White House leaves no room for doubt that he meant it. He and his party are determined to reshape the relationship between Washington and the American people.

The American people, however, have begun to understand what's happening, and that is the beginning of a movement.

———

Traveling around Iowa for most of the 2012 campaign with my friend and advisor Chuck Laudner in his pickup—the "Chuck truck," we called it—rather than a bus and private plane, I had the opportunity to get to know personally so many of the tireless volunteers who make or break a campaign's success. One of them was Wendy Jensen, who epitomized how someone so small and so invisible to national political observers could make a difference.

Wendy volunteered for our campaign in August 2011. She was in her mid-fifties, stood just under five feet tall, and lived in Story County, Iowa, about twenty-five miles north of our headquarters in Urbandale. Because of a medical condition, Wendy couldn't drive, but she was such a devoted worker for our campaign that we would send a member of our staff most mornings to pick her up, and we'd drop her back home at the end of the day.

It was not uncommon for Wendy to make four hundred to five hundred phone calls on our behalf each day. As Christmas approached, she had talked to nearly five thousand voters.

Wendy's secret weapon was her sweetness. After talking with her, no one had the heart to say no to her. She probably was responsible for more converts to our campaign than any other member of our team—including me.

The last time I saw Wendy was at our campaign's Christmas party in mid-December 2011. She was so excited about reaching the five-thousand-call plateau, but as in most of our encounters, all she wanted to talk with me about was my daughter Bella. Wendy had a special heart for others who, like her, struggled with a disabling condition. Over the next couple of days, we didn't hear from Wendy, and we tried unsuccessfully to reach her. We soon learned that she had passed away at home, alone. I was not the only public official at her funeral. Dignitaries from across Iowa came to honor this little lady who selflessly made such a big difference for so many. A tribute to Wendy in the *Iowa Republican* put it best: "Clearly, God needed some extra help in heaven. He brought one of his angels home to help him reach as many hearts as possible...."[1]

At the time of Wendy's passing, the media were focused on pre-caucus polls. I had just received two major endorsements from Iowa officials, which made the front page of national papers and the scroll on the bottom of cable news. Wendy Jensen's name never made the news, but she personified the commitment and devotion that makes a difference not just in politics but in life.

We too often underestimate the difference one person can make, but Wendy showed us what a serious mistake that is. She was not rich in worldly terms, but her gracious demeanor and her tireless commitment to a cause made all the difference in the world—not just for my campaign but for countless of other candidates and causes before me. People like Wendy are being left behind, but they're not asking for help; they're taking action instead.

I'm asked all the time, "I am only one person—what can I do?"

And my answer, with Wendy in mind, is always a single word: "Something."

Do something good for your family, your church, your neighbor, your country, your school, your business, your coworker, the homeless person you pass on the street, or the neighborhood kid who went bad and ended up in prison. And just as important, don't be afraid to stand up for what's right—even if it's uncomfortable, even if you have to pay a price.

One place to start is the public schools. They're supposed to belong to *us*, the people, but we've let activist courts, liberal politicians, and bureaucrats turn them into hostile territory. What book is at the heart of Western civilization and at the heart of the American project? The Bible, of course. Yet it is forbidden to teach from it in most public schools in the land. The most frequently assigned history textbook in American public schools, on the other hand, was written by an anti-American Marxist named Howard Zinn. Do you know if that text is used in your school? The liberal activists, the teachers' unions, and the media do. If you don't, you now have an idea of why they are transforming America right under our noses. I know getting involved is just one more thing that you don't have time for. Got it, but America didn't become unique in human history because our ancestors took the easy path. Self-government isn't easy, and it's not the default setting for human societies. That's why dictators and tyrants have been running most countries for centuries. Real freedom, opportunity, justice, virtue, and security require that we make sacrifices every day to keep them.

Our opponents are revolutionaries. They will always push their agenda. We conservatives are inclined to leave things alone. But every now and then, a generation is asked to step up and fight tyranny. The greatest generation fought the secular statists (Nazis and fascists) across the oceans. Our fight is here at home against a foe whose threat is cleverly disguised and so, in many ways, more dangerous.

We won't win every battle, but fighting for what's right can be its own reward. I have lost many a skirmish only to find out later that the effort was necessary to win a more important battle later. Sometimes my losses were actually victories, but I couldn't see it at the time. Mother Teresa of Calcutta always said, "God has not called me to be successful. He called me to be faithful."

Blue collar conservatives across this country are faithful to a vision that has always defined America but that has been obscured in recent years. We Americans believe in liberty and equal opportunity for all. We believe our leaders should represent 100 percent of Americans. They should not make targets of the wealthy or victims of the poor. We don't believe in economic classes, we believe in economic opportunity, which creates social mobility. We believe that a limited government can help create an environment for all people to prosper morally and economically, thanks to the security provided by the rule of law and balance of powers.

We believe that virtue and civil society are the pillars of freedom. We believe that respecting and honoring faith and family is foundational to freedom. We believe that we are our brother's keeper. We believe in a safety net for people who are struggling, but we don't define compassion by government largesse. We believe compassion is helping another in need. We believe caring should be local, not federal, whenever possible, and temporary, not permanent, or it becomes something that holds people down instead of lifting them up. We believe in upward mobility, not dependency.

We believe that all human beings are created in the image of God and that all life has dignity. We believe that life begins at conception. We believe in justice and fairness. We oppose corruption, cronyism, oppression, and injustice. We believe that work and the ability to provide for one's family through a job is a source of human dignity. We don't look down on any job. America was built by immigrants, and we are for legal immigration. America is a beacon to the world for a reason. We look at every job as a rung on the opportunity ladder.

We believe that we can be self-sufficient in energy. We believe that we can regain our global leadership as a manufacturer. We believe that creativity is key, and that Americans are the most ingenious, resourceful people on earth.

We also believe that elections matter. We believe that people matter and that policies matter. Some policies make it harder to prosper in America, and some policies promote freedom and opportunity and give people a better shot at fulfilling the American Dream. We need to raise our voices and work together so that our policies work for America.

We believe that a healthy family is necessary for a flourishing society. Family is the foundation, the first economy, not something to be tinkered with or redefined by government. Parents, not government, know what's best for children. Faith communities know the best way to practice their faith, and the government should not interfere. Our foundational freedom is religious freedom, freedom of conscience. Entrepreneurs, not government, know how to start businesses and create jobs. Doctors, not government, know what's best for patients. Hardworking taxpayers, not government, know the value of money and how to invest in their future. Parents and teachers, not government or teachers' unions, know the unique learning needs of children.

We believe that America has a future, and we believe it is in our and God's hands.

ACKNOWLEDGMENTS

Two days after I ended my campaign for president in 2012, my media consultant and I met with two senior members of the Romney campaign. When we walked into the meeting, Romney's pollster, Neil Newhouse, handed us a polling presentation and a separate single sheet of paper. He had prepared a PowerPoint summary of their internal polling from Iowa through the final contest in Wisconsin to share with us. It was a kind gesture, since they knew that we had never hired a pollster and so had no internal polling numbers of our own. My calculation was that even if we could afford the poll, we had no money to take advantage of the information, so why bother?

Before Neil got into the full presentation, he was excited to explain what was on that single sheet of paper first. It was the responses to a question from a poll taken four days earlier in Pennsylvania, the next state to hold its primary. Neil had noticed that after February 7, when I swept the Colorado and Minnesota caucuses and the Missouri primary, the afternoon exit polls were consistently underestimating my vote. In fact, before the polls closed in the Alabama and Mississippi primaries, the Drudge Report, among others, ran a story based on afternoon exit polling declaring Romney the winner in Mississippi and running a close second to Newt Gingrich in Alabama. I appeared to be coming in third in both races. That night I won Alabama by 5 percent and Mississippi by 2. So Neil began to ask an additional question in his polling that he had never asked before: "What time are you planning to vote?"

According to the Pennsylvania poll in my hand, people planning to vote before noon favored me by 5 points; those planning to vote between noon and five favored Romney by 4 points; and those who weren't going to vote till after five favored me by 21 points! Working Americans and busy mothers who couldn't get to the polls during the day were voting for me in a big way, making all of the prognosticators look bad on election night.

Although the media never reported it, I knew I had connected with working Americans during the campaign, and not because I had talked about "social issues." The media love to put candidates, particularly culturally conservative candidates, into a box and never under any circumstances let them out. Well, I knew our message was the right message not only to win in November, but to get our country back on the right track.

As I walked back to my car from that meeting with Neil Newhouse, the idea for *Blue Collar Conservatives* began to take shape in my mind. I want to thank Marji Ross and her staff at Regnery for seeing what the media refused to see and asking me to work with them on this project. Thanks in particular to my editors, Tom Spence and Harry Crocker, for their excellent assistance and counsel, and to Katharine Mancuso and Maria Ruhl for their tireless work that kept this project on schedule.

Melissa Anderson and Mark Rodgers, the writing team who have worked on so many projects with me over the years, were extremely helpful in framing the book as well as providing me with tremendous support throughout the research and writing of the text. Thanks also to Ben Kafferlin, who was a great assistant to us all.

Of course, in a life with a more than full-time job and seven children to raise, none of this would be possible without my soul mate and encourager in chief, Karen. During this time she was also engaged in a book project, so her willingness to make time for me is all the more amazing and appreciated.

NOTES

Introduction

1. David Horowitz, "Horowitz: Obama Still Wants to Fundamentally Transform America," *Washington Times*, September 27, 2012, http://www.washingtontimes.com/news/2012/sep/27/obama-still-wants-to-fundamentally-transform-ameri/.

2. John McCormick and Lisa Lerer, "Santorum Says Romney 'Uniquely Unqualified' to Tackle Obama," Bloomberg.com, February 27, 2012, http://www.bloomberg.com/news/2012-02-27/santorum-romney-uniquely-unqualified-to-confront-obama.html.

3. See, for example: "Krauthammer: Romney Will Win, Obama Has Nothing to Run On," Real Clear Politics, July 25, 2012, http://www.

realclearpolitics.com/video/2012/07/25/krauthammer_romney_will_
win_in_november_obama_has_nothing_to_run_on.html.

4.   Henry Olsen, "What Voters Want: A President Who Cares," *New York
Post*, November 9, 2012, http://nypost.com/2012/11/09/what_
voters_want_a_prez_who_cares.

5.   Evann Gastaldo, "*Daily Show*: Romney Like the 'Man Who Fired Your
Dad,'" Newser, December 13, 2011, http://www.newser.com/
story/135301/daily-show-video-mitt-romney-like-the-man-who-just-
fired-your-dad.html.

6.   John F. Kennedy, "Remarks of Senator John F. Kennedy, Municipal
Auditorium, Canton, Ohio," American Presidency Project, University
of California, Santa Barbara, transcript, speech given September 27,
1960, http://www.presidency.ucsb.edu/ws/?pid=74231.

7.   See Pete Wehner, "Demographics and the GOP," Commentary, February 6, 2014, http://www.commentarymagazine.com/2014/02/06/
demographics-and-the-gop/. The citations that follow are to the
sources from which Mr. Wehner drew the data that he assembled in
his posting on Commentary.

8.   Ronald Brownstein, "Bad Bet: Why Republicans Can't Win with Whites
Alone," *National Journal*, September 5, 2013, http://www.national
journal.com/magazine/bad-bet-why-republicans-can-t-win-with-
whites-alone-20130905.

9.   Ibid.

10.   Sean Trende, "The Case of the Missing White Voters, Revisited," Real
Clear Politics, June 21, 2013, http://www.realclearpolitics.com/articles/
2013/06/21/the_case_of_the_missing_white_voters_revisited_118893.
html.

11.   Joel Kotkin, "Off the Rails: How the Party of Lincoln Became the Party
of Plutocrats," New Geography, November 23, 2012, http://www.
newgeography.com/content/003253-off-rails-how-party-lincoln-
became-party-plutocrats.

Chapter 1: Blue Collar Conservatives Really Did Build It

1. Raj Chetty, "Is the United States Still a Land of Opportunity? Recent Trends in Intergenerational Mobility," *Equality of Opportunity Project*, January 2014, http://obs.rc.fas.harvard.edu/chetty/mobility_trends. pdf.

2. Robert Samuelson, "The Social Mobility Muddle," *Washington Post*, January 29, 2014, http://www.washingtonpost.com/opinions/robert-samuelson-the-mobility-muddle/2014/01/29/ad6ebef6-8929-11e3-916e-e01534b1e132_story.html.

3. Nancy Dillon, "Fewer Americans Than Ever Are Getting Married: Poll," *New York Daily News*, December 14, 2011, http://www.nydailynews. com/life-style/health/americans-married-poll-article-1.991402; and Michelle Castillo, "Almost Half of First Babies in U.S. Born to Unwed Mothers," CBS News, March 15, 2013, http://www.cbsnews.com/news/ almost-half-of-first-babies-in-us-born-to-unwed-mothers/.

Chapter 2: Restoring the American Dream for Workers

1. Luigi Zingales, "When Business and Government Are Bedfellows," *Economist*, August 23, 2012, http://www.economist.com/blogs/ prospero/2012/08/quick-study-luigi-zingales-crony-capitalism?zid= 316&ah=2f6fb672faf113fdd3b11cd1b1bf8a77.

2. Zingales, "Crony Capitalism and the Crisis of the West," June 6, 2012, *Wall Street Journal*, http://online.wsj.com/news/articles/SB10001424 052702303665904577450071884712152.

3. James Truslow Adams, *The Epic of America*, reprint (New Jersey: Trans-action Publishers, 2012).

4. Rich Morin and Seth Motel, "A Third of Americans Now Say They Are in the Lower Classes," Pew Research, September 10, 2012, http://www. pewsocialtrends.org/2012/09/10/a-third-of-americans-now-say-they-are-in-the-lower-classes/.

5. Dean Schabner, "Americans Work More Than Anyone," May 1, 2013, ABC News, http://abcnews.go.com/US/story?id=93364.

6. David Lightman, "McClatchy-Marist Poll: American Dream Seen as Out of Reach," February 13, 2014, http://www.mcclatchydc. com/2014/02/13/218026/mcclatchy-marist-poll-american.html.

7. "Post–Miller Center Poll: American Dream and Economic Struggles," *Washington Post*, November 25, 2013, http://www.washingtonpost. com/politics/polling/postmiller-center-poll-american-dream-economic/2013/11/25/b83f1c1a-2892-11e3-8ab3-b5aacc9e1165_page. html.

8. Ron Haskins, Julia B. Isaacs, and Isabel V. Sawhill, *Getting Ahead or Losing Ground: Economic Mobility in America* (Washington, D.C.: Brookings Institution, February 2008), http://www.brookings.edu/ research/reports/2008/02/economic-mobility-sawhill.

9. Kelly Musick and Ann Meier, "Are Both Parents Always Better Than One?," Community and Rural Development Institute, Cornell University, April 2009, http://www.human.cornell.edu/pam/outreach/ upload/parentalconflict.pdf.

10. Ned Smith, "The New Definition of the American Dream," *Business-NewsDaily*, Yahoo!, September 22, 2012, http://news.yahoo.com/ definition-american-dream-105253284.html.

11. Barbara Hollingsworth, "Barbara Walters: 'I Regret Not Having More Children,'" CNS News, December 23, 2013, http://cnsnews.com/news/ article/barbara-hollingsworth/barbara-walters-i-regret-not-having-more-children.

12. Julia La Roche, "Warren Buffett: This Is How You Know You're Really Successful," Business Insider, May 2, 2013, http://www.businessinsider. com/live-warren-buffett-talking-about-women-and-work-2013-5.

13. Sarah Burd-Sharps and Kristen Lewis, *One in Seven: Ranking Youth Disconnection in the 25 Largest Metro Areas*, Measure of America, September 2012, http://www.measureofamerica.org/wp-content/ uploads/2012/09/MOA-One_in_Seven09-14.pdf.

Chapter 3: A GOP That
Stands Up for Everyone

1. "History of Federal Individual Income Bottom and Top Bracket Rates,"
    National Taxpayers Union, accessed February 2014, http://www.ntu.
    org/tax-basics/history-of-federal-individual-1.html.

2. "College Enrollment and Work Activity of 2012 High School Gradu-
    ates," Bureau of Labor Statistics, April 17, 2013, http://www.bls.gov/
    news.release/hsgec.nr0.htm.

3. Stephanie J. Ventura, "Changing Patterns of Nonmarital Childbearing
    in the United States," Centers for Disease Control and Prevention, May
    2009, http://www.cdc.gov/nchs/data/databriefs/db18.htm; and Joyce
    A. Martin, "Births: Final Data for 2010," *National Vital Statistics Report*,
    Centers for Disease Control and Prevention, August 18, 2012, http://
    www.cdc.gov/nchs/data/nvsr/nvsr61/nvsr61_01.pdf.

4. Ana Marie Cox, "The Amazing Reformation of Mitt and Ann Rom-
    ney," Awl, December 5, 2012, http://www.theawl.com/2012/12/the-
    amazing-reformation-of-mitt-and-ann-romney.

5. Charities Aid Foundation, "World Giving Index 2013," Charities Aid
    Foundation Online, December 2013, https://www.cafonline.org/PDF/
    WorldGivingIndex2013_1374AWEB.pdf.

6. Arthur Brooks, *Who Really Cares: The Surprising Truth About Compas-
    sionate Conservatism* (New York: Basic Books, 2007).

7. Josh Gerstein, "Romney 2011 Taxes: Mitt Gives More to Charity Than
    President Obama, Joe Biden," Politico, September 21, 2012, http://
    www.politico.com/news/stories/0912/81529.html.

8. Republican National Committee, "Republican Platform of 1856,"
    American Presidency Project, June 18, 1856, http://www.presidency.
    ucsb.edu/ws/?pid=29619; and "House Vote #182 IN 1964," Govtrack.
    us, July 2, 1964, https://www.govtrack.us/congress/votes/88-1964/
    h182.

9. David Catron, "Republicans and Women's Rights: A Brief Reality
    Check," *American Spectator*, April 30, 2012, http://spectator.org/
    articles/35608/republicans-and-womens-rights-brief-reality-check;
    and "The Passage of the 19th Amendment," *New York Times*, June 5,

1919, available on the Modern History Sourcebook, Fordham University, http://www.fordham.edu/halsall/mod/1920womensvote.html.

Chapter 4: Holes in the Boat

1.   Kathie Obradovich, "Does a Rising Tide Lift All Boats? Santorum Challenges GOP Economic Focus," *Iowa Politics* (blog), DesMoinesRegister.com, August 10, 2013, http://blogs.desmoinesregister.com/dmr/index.php/2013/08/10/does-a-rising-tide-lift-all-boats-santorum-challenges-gop-econmic-focus/article.

2.   Nathan Lewis, "Flat Tax vs. Fair Tax vs. Herman Cain's 9-9-9 Plan," *Forbes*, October 13, 2011, http://www.forbes.com/sites/nathan-lewis/2011/10/13/flat-tax-vs-fair-tax-vs-herman-cains-9-9-9-plan/.

3.   Richard Ebeling, "The Lasting Legacy of the Reagan Revolution," *Free-man*, Foundation for Economic Education, July 1, 2004, http://www.fee.org/the_freeman/detail/the-lasting-legacy-of-the-reagan-revolution.

4.   Associated Press, "Widening Income Gap Hurts Economy, Survey Says," NBC News, December 18, 2013, http://www.nbcnews.com/business/widening-income-gap-hurting-economy-survey-says-2D11767020; and "School Enrollment," U.S. Census Bureau, October 2012, accessed January 29, 2014, http://www.census.gov/hhes/school/data/cps/2012/tables.html.

5.   "Reagan Government Is Not the Solution to Our Problem, Government Is the Problem," YouTube video, from Ronald Reagan's first inaugural address, uploaded February 4, 2009, by "deck0930," accessed January 29, 2014, http://www.youtube.com/watch?v=6ixNPplo-SU.

6.   James Sherk, "Not Looking for Work: Why Labor Force Participation Has Fallen during the Recession," Backgrounder Update 2722, Heritage Foundation, September 5, 2013, http://www.heritage.org/research/reports/2013/09/not-looking-for-work-why-labor-force-participation-has-fallen-during-the-recession.

7.   "Income Inequality Grew Faster under Obama, according to One Measure," Huffington Post, September 1, 2013, http://www. huffingtonpost.com/2013/09/01income-inequality-obama_n_ 3853183.html; and Morgan Korn, "More Proof That the Rich Are Getting Richer and the Poor Poorer," Daily Ticker, Yahoo! Finance, October 10, 2013, http://finance.yahoo.com/blogs/daily-ticker/more-proof-rich-getting-richer-poor-poorer-154916333.html.

8.   Associated Press, "Widening Income Gap Hurts Economy, Survey Says."

9.   David Brodwin, "Suffering under the Weight of Inequality," *Economic Intelligence* (blog), *U.S. News & World Report*, September 12, 2013, http://www.usnews.com/opinion/blogs/economic-intelligence/ 2013/09/12/record-high-income-inequality-threatens-us-growth.

10. Annie Lowrey, "The Rich Get Richer through the Recovery," *Economix* (blog), *New York Times*, September 10, 2013, http://economix.blogs. nytimes.com/2013/09/10/the-rich-get-richer-through-the-recovery/?_ r=0.

11. Ibid.

12. Peter Morici, "Extended Unemployment Benefits Slow Growth," United Press International, January 6, 2014, http://www.upi.com/Top_News/ Analysis/Outside-View/2014/01/06/Extended-unemployment-benefits-slow-growth/UPI-25761389026285/.

13. "Unemployment in October 2009," Bureau of Labor Statistics, November 10, 2009, accessed January 29, 2014, http://www.bls.gov/opub/ ted/2009/ted_20091110.htm.

14. "Average Duration of Unemployment," Economic Research, Federal Reserve Bank of St. Louis, accessed January 29, 2014, http://research. stlouisfed.org/fred2/graph/?s[1][id]=UEMPMEAN#.

15. Stephen A. Wandner and Thomas Stengle, "Unemployment Insurance: Measuring Who Receives It," Bureau of Labor Statistics, July 1997, accessed January 29, 2014, http://stats.bls.gov/mlr/1997/07/art2full. pdf.

16. Rob Valletta and Katherine Kuang, "Extended Unemployment and UI Benefits," Federal Reserve Bank of San Francisco, April 19, 2010, accessed January 29, 2014, http://www.frbsf.org/economic-research/

publications/economic-letter/2010/april/extended-unemployment-insurance-benefits/.

17. John C. Ogg, "Twelve Things Not to Do If You Win the Lottery," *USA Today*, August 25, 2013, http://www.usatoday.com/story/money/personalfinance/2013/08/25/what-not-to-do-lottery-winners/2696845/.

18. Glenn Grotham, "America's Biggest Problem: The Breakdown of the Family," accessed January 29, 2014, http://legis.wisconsin.gov/senate/grothman/Documents/Grothman-families.pdf.

19. Nicholas Kristof, "Profiting from a Child's Illiteracy," *New York Times*, December 7, 2012, http://www.nytimes.com/2012/12/09/opinion/sunday/kristof-profiting-from-a-childs-illiteracy.html?pagewanted=all.

20. Doug McKelway, "Widespread Fraud Reported in Social Security Administration's Disability Program," Fox News, October 8, 2013, http://www.foxnews.com/politics/2013/10/08/widespread-fraud-reported-in-social-security-administration-disability-program/.

21. Robert Rector, "Obama's End Run on Welfare Reform, Part Two: Dismantling Workfare," Heritage Foundation, September 26, 2012, http://www.heritage.org/research/reports/2012/09/obamas-end-run-on-welfare-reform-part-two-dismantling-workfare.

22. Charles Murray, "A New Kind of Segregation," chapter 3 in *Coming Apart: The State of White America, 1960–2010* (New York: Crown Forum, 2012).

23. Ibid.

24. Ron Haskins, "Combating Poverty: Understanding New Challenges for Families," Brookings Institution, June 5, 2012, http://www.brookings.edu/research/testimony/2012/06/05-poverty-families-haskins.

25. Daniel Halper, "Food Stamp Growth 75x Greater Than Job Creation," *Weekly Standard*, November 2, 2012, accessed January 29, 2014, http://www.weeklystandard.com/blogs/food-stamp-growth-75x-greater-job-creation_660073.html.

Chapter 5: Renewing
the Pursuit of Happiness

1. See John G. West, "The Evangelical Voter," *First Things*, February 2013; and Rich Exner, "Ohio Voter Registration and 2012 Turnout by County," Cleveland.com, November 15, 2012, http://www.cleveland.com/datacentral/index.ssf/2012/11/ohio_voting_registration_and_2.html.

2. Proverbs 29:18, KJV.

3. Brittany Wong, "Money and Divorce: What Recent Divorce Research Has to Say about Poverty's Effect on Marriage," Huffington Post, August 8, 2012, http://www.huffingtonpost.com/2012/08/29/poverty-and-divorce_n_1826433.html.

4. "Statistics," Fatherless Generation, accessed January 29, 2014, http://thefatherlessgeneration.wordpress.com/statistics/.

5. Alison Acosta Fraser, "Federal Spending by the Numbers, 2012," Special Report 121, Heritage Foundation, October 16, 2012, http://www.heritage.org/research/reports/2012/10/federal-spending-by-the-numbers-2012.

6. "History," Center for Social Justice, accessed January 29, 2014, http://www.centreforsocialjustice.org.uk/about-us/history.

7. Ibid.

8. *Encyclopedia Britannica: A Dictionary of Arts, Sciences, and General Literature*, vol. 9, s.v. "Fletcher, Andrew" (Philadelphia: Maxwell Sommerville: 1894), 264–65.

9. *Webster's Revised Unabridged Dictionary (1913 + 1828)*, s.v. "Happiness," available online at the ARTFL Project, http://machaut.uchicago.edu/?action=search&resource=Webster%27s&word=Happiness&quicksearch=on.

10. *Webster's 1828 English Dictionary*, s.v. "Good," available online at Sorabji.com, http://sorabji.com/1828/words/g/good.html.

Chapter 6: Government Cannot Read You a Bedtime Story

1. Robert Rector, "Marriage: America's Greatest Weapon against Child Poverty," Special Report no. 117, Heritage Foundation, September 5, 2012, http://www.heritage.org/research/reports/2012/09/marriage-americas-greatest-weapon-against-child-poverty.

2. Center for Health Statistics, "FastStats: Unmarried Childbearing," Centers for Disease Control and Prevention, updated August 5, 2013, http://www.cdc.gov/nchs/fastats/unmarry.htm.

3. Hope Yen, "4.1 Million Single-Mother Families Are Living in Poverty: Census," Huffington Post, September 19, 2013, http://www.huffingtonpost.com/2013/09/19/single-mother-poverty_n_3953047.html.

4. Daniel P. Moynihan, *The Negro Family: The Case for National Action* (Washington, D.C.: Office of Policy Planning and Research, U.S. Department of Labor, 1965).

5. Steven Nelson, "Census Bureau Links Poverty with Out-of-Wedlock Births," *U.S. News & World Report*, May 6, 2013, http://www.usnews.com/news/newsgram/articles/2013/05/06/census-bureau-links-poverty-with-out-of-wedlock-births.

6. Ann Hornaday, "Spike Lee Talks about 'Red Hook Summer,'" *Washington Post*, August 24, 2012, http://www.washingtonpost.com/lifestyle/style/spike-lee-talks-about-red-hook-summer/2012/08/22/ff4d8c24-ec78-11e1-a80b-9f898562d010_story.html.

7. Zeke J. Miller, "Obama Discusses Race, Fatherhood, Responsibility (Transcript Included)," *Swampland* (blog), *Time*, May 19, 2013, http://swampland.time.com/2013/05/19/obama-discusses-race-responsibility-at-morehouse-college/#ixzz2loT2WvhU.

8. Robert Rector, "Understanding Illegitimacy," Heritage Foundation, April 12, 2010, http://www.heritage.org/research/commentary/2010/04/understanding-illegitimacy.

9. Mona Charen, "The Inequality of Marriage-Culture Collapse," *National Review Online*, http://www.nationalreview.com/article/370240/inequality-marriage-culture-collapse-mona-charen.

10.   Katie Reilly, "Sesame Street Reaches Out to 2.7 Million American Children with an Incarcerated Parent," Pew Research Center, June 21, 2013, http://www.pewresearch.org/fact-tank/2013/06/21/sesame-street-reaches-out-to-2-7-million-american-children-with-an-incarcerated-parent/; and "You Commit Three Felonies a Day," *Wall Street Journal*, September 27, 2009, http://online.wsj.com/news/articles/SB1000142 4052748704471504574438900830760842.

11.   National Vital Statistics System, "National Marriage and Divorce Rate Trends," Centers for Disease Control and Prevention, February 19, 2013, http://www.cdc.gov/nchs/nvss/marriage_divorce_tables.htm.

12.   "MSNBC Host Melissa Harris-Perry," YouTube video, recording of "Lean Forward" commercial, uploaded April 4, 2013, by "yazchat," http://www.youtube.com/watch?v=N3qtpdSQox0.

13.   As quoted in Isabel Sawhill, "20 Years Later, It Turns Out Dan Quayle Was Right about Murphy Brown and Unmarried Moms," *Washington Post*, May 25, 2012, http://www.washingtonpost.com/opinions/20-years-later-it-turns-out-dan-quayle-was-right-about-murphy-brown-and-unmarried-moms/2012/05/25/gJQAsNCJqU_story.html.

14.   Jonah Goldberg, "Goldberg: The Wisdom of Dan Quayle," *Los Angeles Times*, March 26, 2013, http://www.latimes.com/news/science/la-oe-goldberg-murphy-brown-families-20130326,0,771523. column#axzz2kIaHVml6.

15.   Patrick F. Fagan, "Why Religion Matters Even More: The Impact of Religious Practice on Social Stability," Backgrounder no. 1992, Heritage Foundation, December 18, 2006, http://www.heritage.org/research/reports/2006/12/why-religion-matters-even-more-the-impact-of-religious-practice-on-social-stability.

Chapter 7: Replace Obamacare Before It's Too Late

1.   Chris Fleming, "2009 U.S. Health Spending Estimated at 2.5 Trillion," Health Affairs, February 4, 2010, http://healthaffairs.org/blog/2010/02/04/2009-u-s-health-spending-estimated-at-2-5-trillion/.

2. Paul Krugman, "Clinton, Obama, Insurance," *New York Times*, February 4, 2008, http://www.nytimes.com/2008/02/04/opinion/04krugman. html?_r=0.

3. Sarah Kliff, "Obamacare Leaves Millions Uninsured: Here's Who They Are," *Washington Post*, June 7, 2013, http://www.washingtonpost.com/ blogs/wonkblog/wp/2013/06/07/obamacare-leaves-millions-uninsured-heres-who-they-are/.

4. Ezra Klein, "Wonkbook: 40 Percent of Obamacare's IT Isn't Even Built Yet," *Washington Post*, November 20, 2013, http://www.washingtonpost. com/blogs/wonkblog/wp/2013/11/20/wonkbook-40-percent-of-obamacares-it-isnt-even-built-yet/.

5. Eric Pianin, "Top Tier Hospitals Excluded from Obamacare," Yahoo! Finance, December 9, 2013, http://finance.yahoo.com/news/top-tier-hospitals-excluded-obamacare-191700528.html.

6. Angie Drobnic Holan, "Lie of the Year: 'If You Like Your Health Care Plan, You Can Keep It,'" Politifact, December 12, 2013, http://www. politifact.com/truth-o-meter/article/2013/dec/12/lie-year-if-you-like-your-health-care-plan-keep-it/.

7. Glenn Kessler, "The GOP Claim That More Americans Have Lost Insurance Than Gained It under Obamacare," *Washington Post*, January 6, 2014, http://www.washingtonpost.com/blogs/fact-checker/wp/ 2014/01/06/the-gop-claim-that-more-americans-have-lost-insurance-than-gained-it-under-obamacare/.

8. Jenna Levy, "In US, Uninsured Rate Shows Initial Decline in 2014," Gallup, January 23, 2014, http://www.gallup.com/poll/166982/ uninsured-rate-shows-initial-decline-2014.aspx.

9. Cole Waterman, "Denied Obamacare Coverage, Michigan Family with Disabilities Finds Alternatives Much More Expensive," MLive.com, January 21, 2014, http://www.mlive.com/news/bay-city/index. ssf/2014/01/bangor_township_family_says_he.html.

10. Doug McKelway, "Obamacare Forcing People into Medicaid," Fox News, January 22, 2014, http://www.foxnews.com/politics/2013/11/22/ obamacare-forcing-people-into-medicaid/.

11. Nicole Hopkins, "ObamaCare Forced Mom into Medicaid," *Wall Street Journal*, November 20, 2013, http://online.wsj.com/news/articles/SB1 0001424052702303531204579207724152219590.

12. *2012 State of Well-Being: Community, State and Congressional District Well-Being Reports; Iowa* (Gallup and Healthways, 2013), http://cdn1. hubspot.com/hub/162029/WBI2012/Iowa_2012_State_Report.pdf.

13. "South Carolina Birth Outcomes Initiative Celebrates Success," press release, South Carolina Institute of Medicine & Public Health, January 2014, http://imph.org/south-carolina-birth-outcomes-initiative-celebrates-success/.

14. Yvonne Zipp, "Stryker Corp. to Complete Planned Layoffs of 1,000 Workers by End of 2012," MLive.com, November 19, 2012, http://www. mlive.com/business/west-michigan/index.ssf/2012/11/stryker_corp_ to_complete_layof.html.

15. "Cook Medical Shelves Plans to Open Five News Plants in the Next Five Years," *Canton Daily Ledger*, August 1, 2012, http://www.canton dailyledger.com/article/20120801/NEWS/308019977.

16. Tom Gara, "Union Letter: Obamacare Will 'Destroy the Very Health and Wellbeing' of Workers," *Wall Street Journal*, July 12, 2013, http://blogs. wsj.com/corporate-intelligence/2013/07/12/union-letter-obamacare-will-destroy-the-very-health-and-wellbeing-of-workers/.

17. Betsy McCaughey, *Beating Obamacare, 2014* (Washington, D.C.: Regnery, 2014), 53.

18. Howard Dean, "The Affordable Care Act's Rate-Setting Won't Work," *Wall Street Journal*, July 28, 2013, http://online.wsj.com/news/articles/ SB10001424127887324110404578628542498014414.

Chapter 8: Innovating and Personalizing Education

1. Rick Santorum, "Vision & Values: Goodness and Greatness," Center for Vision & Values, Grove City College, transcript, speech given May 1, 1998, http://www.visionandvalues.org/1998/05/vision-a-values-goodness-and-greatness/.

2. See the Common Core State Standards Mission Statement: http://
    www.corestandards.org/.

3. Lyndsey Layton, "National Public High School Graduation Rate at a
    Four-Decade High," *Washington Post*, January 22, 2013, http://articles.
    washingtonpost.com/2013-01-22/local/36472838_1_graduation-rate-
    dropout-rate-asian-students.

4. "Mathematics: National Results," The Nation's Report Card, 2011,
    National Association of Education Progress, accessed January 29, 2014,
    http://nationsreportcard.gov/math_2011/summary.aspx#; and "Read-
    ing: National Results," The Nation's Report Card, 2011, accessed Janu-
    ary 29, 2014, http://nationsreportcard.gov/reading_2011/summary.
    aspx#.

5. Sally Lovejoy and Chad Miller, "Collective Bargaining and Student
    Academic Achievement," American Action Forum, June 2013, http://
    americanactionforum.org/sites/default/files/Collective%20Bargaining.
    pdf.

6. "College Participation Rates: Percent of 18- to 24-Year-Olds Enrolled
    in College," NCHEMS Information Center, 2009, accessed January 29,
    2014, http://www.higheredinfo.org/dbrowser/index.
    php?measure=104.

7. Society for Human Resource Management Poll, cited in Glenn
    Thompson, "Join the Congressional Career & Technical Education
    Caucus," Dear Colleague Letter, accessed January 29, 2014, https://
    www.acteonline.org/uploadedFiles/Assets_and_Documents/Global/
    files/Policy/CTEDearColleague113.pdf. See also Cassandria Dortch,
    Career and Technical Education (CTE): A Primer (Washington, D.C.:
    Congressional Research Service, September 20, 2012).

Chapter 9: Giving the
American Worker a Fighting Chance

1. Christopher Goodman, "Employment Loss and the 2007–09 Reces-
    sion: An Overview," Bureau of Labor Statistics, April 2011, accessed
    January 29, 2014, http://www.bls.gov/opub/mlr/2011/04/art1full.pdf.

2.   Douglas McIntyre, "North Dakota Jobless Rate at 2.6%," 24/7 Wall St., January 29, 2014, http://247wallst.com/economy/2014/01/29/north-dakota-jobless-rate-at-2-6/.

3.   President Barack Obama, State of the Union address, January 25, 2012.

4.   "Local Area Unemployment Statistics," Bureau of Labor Statistics, December 2013, accessed January 29, 2014, http://www.bls.gov/web/laus/laumstrk.htm.

5.   Jim Snyder, "Obama Pushes Natural-Gas Fracking to Create 600,000 U.S. Jobs," Bloomberg.com News, January 25, 2012, http://www.bloomberg.com/news/2012-01-25/obama-backs-fracking-to-create-600-000-jobs-vows-safe-drilling.html.

6.   Rob Bluey, "Video: Victims of the Obama Drilling Moratorium," Heritage Foundation, May 24, 2011, http://blog.heritage.org/2011/05/24/video-victims-of-the-obama-drilling-moratorium/.

7.   Rebecca Rolfes, "What's It Worth to You?" MSCI, http://forward.msci.org/articles/?id=57.

8.   Ibid.

9.   James L. Gattuso, "Red Tape Rising: A 2011 Mid-Year Report," Heritage Foundation, July 25, 2011, http://www.heritage.org/research/reports/2011/07/red-tape-rising-a-2011-mid-year-report.

Chapter 10: Raising Hope
instead of Taxes

1.   Rick Shenkmen, "When Did Social Security Become the Third Rail of American Politics?," History News Network, http://hnn.us/article/10522.

2.   Emily Brandon, "4 Changes to Social Security Coming in 2011," *U.S. News & World Report*, January 18, 2011, http://money.usnews.com/money/retirement/articles/2011/01/18/4-social-security-changes-coming-in-2011.

3.   "Status of the Social Security and Medicare Programs," Social Security Administration, 2013, accessed January 29, 2014, http://www.ssa.gov/oact/trsum/.

4.   "Rick Santorum on Social Security," On The Issues, March 7, 2012,
      http://www.ontheissues.org/2012/Rick_Santorum_Social_Security.
      htm.

5.   Doug Short, "U.S. Median Household Incomes by Age Bracket:
      1967–2012," Advisor Perspectives, September 17, 2013, http://www.
      advisorperspectives.com/dshort/updates/Household-Incomes-by-
      Age-Brackets.php.

6.   "National Health Expenditures 2012 Highlights," Centers for Medicare
      & Medicaid Services, January 18, 2011, accessed January 29, 2014,
      http://www.cms.gov/Research-Statistics-Data-and-Systems/Statistics-
      Trends-and-Reports/NationalHealthExpendData/downloads/
      highlights.pdf.

7.   Grace-Marie Turner, "Part D Can Be a Model for Medicare Reform,"
      Hill, March 14, 2013, http://thehill.com/blogs/congress-blog/
      healthcare/288147-part-d-can-be-a-model-for-medicare-reform;
      Doug Schoen, "Medicare Part D Continues to Improve Access to
      Drugs," *Forbes*, August 9, 2013, http://www.forbes.com/sites/doug-
      schoen/2013/08/09/medicare-part-d-continues-to-improve-access-
      to-drugs/; and "Medicare Spending and Financing Fact Sheet," Kaiser
      Family Foundation, November 14, 2012, http://kff.org/medicare/
      fact-sheet/medicare-spending-and-financing-fact-sheet/.

8.   Richard Finger, "Fraud and Disability Equal a Multibillion Dollar Black
      Hole for Tax Payers," *Forbes*, January 14, 2013, http://www.forbes.
      com/sites/richardfinger/2013/01/14/fraud-and-disability-equal-a-
      multibillion-dollar-balck-hole-for-taxpayers/.

9.   Thomas Jefferson, "Inaugural Address," transcript, speech given March
      4, 1801, available online through Georgia Tech, http://ahp.gatech.edu/
      jefferson_inaug_1801.html.

10.   Michael Gerson and Peter Wehner, "A Conservative Vision of Govern-
      ment," *National Affairs*, no. 18, Winter 2014, eppc.us4.list-manage.
      com/track/click?u=be333e74ea841be93db60da61&id=8b359623a7&
      e=ef43c68b76.

11.   Tom A. Coburn, *Department of Everything*, November 2012, http://
      www.coburn.senate.gov/public/index.cfm?a=Files.Serve&File_
      id=00783b5a-f0fe-4f80-90d6-019695e52d2d.

12. Christopher Bedford, "Hagel to Shrink Army to Pre-WWII Level," Daily Caller, February 24, 2014, http://dailycaller.com/2014/02/24/ hagel-to-shrink-army-to-pre-wwii-level/.

13. See FairTax.org.

14. Blake Ellis, "4 Tax Breaks for Parents on the Chopping Block," CNN Money, October 11, 2012, http://money.cnn.com/2012/10/11/pf/taxes/ tax-breaks-parents/.

15. Annalyn Kurtz, "Baby Bust: U.S. Births at Record Low," CNN Money, September 6, 2013, http://money.cnn.com/2013/09/06/news/ economy/birth-rate-low/.

Chapter 11: Believing in America's Future

1. Kevin Hall, "Iowa GOP Mourns Passing of Super Volunteer Wendy Jensen," Iowa Republican, December 17, 2011, http://theiowarepublican. com/2011/iowa-gop-mourns-passing-of-super-volunteer-wendy- jensen/.

INDEX